Spiritual Masters Series

T0169212

World Wisdom
The Library of Perennial Philosophy

The Library of Perennial Philosophy is dedicated to the exposition of the timeless Truth underlying the diverse religions. This Truth, often referred to as the *Sophia Perennis*—or Perennial Wisdom—finds its expression in the revealed Scriptures as well as the writings of the great sages and the artistic creations of the traditional worlds.

The Perennial Philosophy provides the intellectual principles capable of explaining both the formal contradictions and the transcendent unity of the great religions.

Ranging from the writings of the great sages of the past, to the perennialist authors of our time, each series of our Library has a different focus. As a whole, they express the inner unanimity, transforming radiance, and irreplaceable values of the great spiritual traditions.

The Laughing Buddha of Tofukuji: The Life of Zen Master Keido Fukushima appears as one of our selections in the Spiritual Masters: East & West series.

Spiritual Masters: East & West Series

This series presents the writings of great spiritual masters of the past and present from both East and West. Carefully selected essential writings of these sages are combined with biographical information, glossaries of technical terms, historical maps, and pictorial and photographic art in order to communicate a sense of their respective spiritual climates.

THE LAUGHING BUDDHA OF TOFUKUJI:

THE LIFE OF ZEN MASTER KEIDO FUKUSHIMA

BY

ISHWAR C. HARRIS

FOREWORD BY

JEFF SHORE

World Wisdom

The Laughing Buddha of Tofukuji: The Life of Zen Master Keido
Fukushima
© 2004 World Wisdom, Inc.

Library of Congress Cataloging-in-Publication Data

Harris, Ishwar c., 1943-
  The laughing Buddha of Tofukuji: the life of Zen master Keido Fukushima
/ Ishwar C. Harris, Jeff Shore.
      p. cm. – (Spiritual masters. East and West series)
  Includes bibliographical references.
  ISBN 0-941532-62-3 (pbk. : alk. paper)
  1. Fukushima, Keido, 1933- 2. Priests, Zen–Japan–Biography. I. Shore, Jeff.
II. Title. III. Series.
  BQ956.K8774H37 2004
  294.3'927'092–dc22

                                                              2004017535

Printed on acid-free paper in Canada

For information address World Wisdom, Inc.
P.O. Box 2682, Bloomington, Indiana 47402-2682

www.worldwisdom.com

For all my teachers
in India, Japan, and the United States,
including
Roshi Keido Fukushima

Table of Contents

Foreword

Whether you have known Keido Fukushima for decades or are encountering him for the first time through the pages of this intimate portrait, we all have the pleasure of meeting him as if he were an old and dear friend. Samples of his calligraphy provide further glimpses into the heart and mind of a leading Zen master of the modern world.

Roshi Fukushima, as the Japanese Zen master is called, is generally sparing with personal details of his life. Even old friends of his, however, will be surprised by some of the revelations Professor Ishwar Harris has managed to uncover and share with us in this volume. Through these intimate details the reader can feel the pulse of a Zen master as a flesh-and-blood human being. We can see into the heart of a man who happens to be a Zen master. This approach provides an extraordinary occasion to come into touch with Zen Buddhism through one modern master's life, love, and laughter.

The Zen Buddhist tradition, as Professor Harris mentions, is said to begin with the selfless smile of Buddha's disciple Mahakasyapa. Zen springs to life when we share the joy of this "open secret." See if you don't find yourself breaking into a broad smile and beaming with delight every now and then as you read through this account.

Even more importantly though, in these pages we are given the chance to see something of ourselves. Having opened this book, open yourself. I trust you'll find something oddly familiar, yet refreshingly new. Dig right in!

Jeff Shore
Lay Zen man
Professor of International Zen
Hanazono University
Kyoto, Japan

Preface

This work is as much about understanding Zen as it is about understanding the life and work of the Zen master, Keido Fukushima. I first came into contact with him in 1973 at Claremont Graduate School in southern California. He was a Rinzai Zen monk, struggling to learn English, and I was a graduate student struggling to complete my formal education. We shared a common house which facilitated our friendship, a relationship that has continued to the present. I have learned more about Zen by observing his life than by reading books about Zen.

Since 1980 when Keido became the Zen master of Tofukuji monastery in Kyoto, Japan, he has trained over one hundred Zen monks, lectured to thousands of students in America, produced countless works of Zen calligraphy, made disciples both in Japan and the United States, written books on Zen, and is helping to restore Rinzai Zen tradition in China. His friends gravitate to him due to his friendliness, compassion, and generosity. Those who meet him for the first time are attracted to his smile, which is contagious. His disciples hail him as a master *koan* trainer whose deep penetrating insight has awakened in them an awareness of Zen. By his own admission, he was fortunate enough to train with Japan's two well-known Zen masters, i.e., Roshi Okada and Roshi Shibayama.

D. T. Suzuki, a Zen scholar, who is well known in the West for interpreting Zen to western audiences through his writings on Zen, has been a major force behind Keido Fukushima's travels to the United States. It was D. T. Suzuki who recommended to Columbia University that it should invite Roshi Shibayama to give annual Zen lectures at Columbia after Suzuki retired. As Shibayama undertook this task, he groomed his disciple Keido, to follow in his footsteps. For more than twenty years, Keido Fukushima has brought Zen understanding to American students, following the legacy of Shibayama and D. T. Suzuki. He is among the few Japanese Zen masters who has a good grasp of the English language and can communicate well with his audience.

Roshi Keido Fukushima sees himself as a harbinger of "International Zen." As a bridge-builder between the East and West, he foresees his mission to integrate the best of western values with that of the East. In this process he does not want to dilute the "essential Zen" and accommodate it to the needs of the American people. He is critical of those Zen teachers who popularize Zen by making it appealing to their western audiences. For Keido, they are producing "weak Zen," which is detrimental to spiritual growth. His mission is to expose a pristine Zen to the people in the West. In order to accomplish this task he has taken a special interest in college and university students. He has established a unique connection between his monastery, Tofukuji, and several American colleges. Under this program, the American students are invited to spend short or long terms practicing Zen at his monastery in Kyoto. So far many students have made this journey.

The present book is a story of the Zen master Keido Fukushima's life and his accomplishments. It shows how a living Zen master applies Zen in his life. It summarizes his teachings in a manner that is accessible to a lay reader as well as to a student of Zen Buddhism. In the spirit of one of Keido's calligraphy pieces in English, "Watch, Touch, and Bite," it is an invitation to befriend Fukushima and to taste his brand of Zen.

Ishwar C. Harris
The Synod Professor of Religious Studies
The College of Wooster
Wooster, Ohio

Acknowledgments

The present work would have remained incomplete had I not received support and cooperation from many individuals who graciously extended their helping hands to me from time to time. I am indebted for their encouragement, thoughtfulness, and friendship.

First and foremost I am grateful to Roshi Keido Fukushima for permitting me to stay at his monastery and to participate in the monastic life of Tofukuji. Furthermore, I thank him for finding time from his busy schedule to talk with me about his life and thought. I trust that I have accurately presented his ideas in this book. Any mistakes or misconceptions are due to faults of my own.

In particular I am thankful to Professor Jeff Shore of Hanazono University in Kyoto and a friend of Tofukuji. His encouragement and thoughtful suggestions made this work easier. Not only that, he was kind enough to correct my mistakes and provide me with pertinent information necessary for this work. It was only appropriate to ask him to write a foreword for this book, which he has thoughtfully provided.

Thanks are also due to Dr. Peggy Dornish, Professor Emeritus, Pomona College for providing correct information incorporated in the Prologue. If it had not been for her efforts to bring Keido Fukushima to Claremont, perhaps many of us would never have met him, and the possibility of writing a biography of him would never have entered my mind.

When I was discouraged that, due to his busy schedule, I might not see the Roshi for weeks, his administrative assistant, Kei-san, came to my rescue. He assured me that he would plead with the Zen master on my behalf and find time in his schedule. I thank him for keeping his promise. I also thank him for looking after my needs during the months I stayed in the monastery. As for the monks of Tofukuji, I cannot thank them enough for accepting me into their community. I will be forever in their debt for teaching me how to behave properly in a monastery.

My two extended trips to Japan were supported by various grants. I am thankful to Earlham College's Japan Study Office for awarding me two separate grants to stay in Japan. The College of Wooster's Leaves Program permitted me to leave the campus, and the Henry Luce III Fund for Distinguished Scholarship, supervised by the College, further supported my research. I am thankful to the College of Wooster for the support of my work.

Kathie Clyde, one of the administrative assistants at the College of Wooster, efficiently completed the tedious job of typing the manuscript. I thank Kathie for staying with this project from the beginning until the end, even though sometimes it meant readjusting her schedule.

I am totally indebted to the contributors of the Impression section toward the end of this book. I am thankful they agreed to write on behalf of the Zen master, and also found time to complete the job. Thank you Stephen Addiss, Tim Armacost, Hannalori Bates, Paul F. Knitter, Jay McDaniel, Ginny Miraldi, Andrea S. Norris, Barbara Ruch, Jeff Shore, Hap Tivey, Mary Evelyn Tucker, and Alexander Vesey.

Thanks are properly due to Barry McDonald, Managing Director of World Wisdom. His encouraging comments about the importance of this project made me take this work seriously and complete it on schedule. Also, thank you Susana Marin, Graphic Designer at World Wisdom, for so creatively designing the cover and accepting my suggestions.

My wife, Jyotsna, and my daughters, Meera and Anjali, have lovingly tolerated my absence from home in connection with the research associated with this work, and indeed, all of my work. I thank my family for their support and understanding, and for occasionally entertaining Roshi Fukushima and his party in our home.

Roshi Keido Fukushima

Prologue

It was a pleasant sunny afternoon when some of us, students at Claremont Graduate School, gathered at Ontario Airport in southern California to bid goodbye to Keido Fukushima. We knew him as Gensho, a Zen monk, who had spent a memorable year with us at the Blaisdell Institute for World Religions and Cultures. Amidst the sadness we felt to see him go, it was his smile and constant joking that kept us laughing and lighthearted at the airport. In those days there were no security checks and air marshals with which to contend. We had congregated outside the terminal, his plane in sight. We shook hands and watched as he made his way on the open tarmac toward the plane. He climbed the stairs and, just before boarding, turned around and with a big smile yelled, "Sayonara," then disappeared. As many of his friends departed, I stayed with a few of his other close friends until the plane took off. At least one woman had tears in her eyes. I felt a strange sadness. The year was 1973.

I believed I would never see Gensho again. The thought of writing his biography never even entered my mind. On the way back from the airport, I kept thinking how deeply he had touched my life. My thoughts went back to the day when the director of the Blaisdell Institute had informed us that a Zen monk would be coming to live with us for a year at Blaisdell House. "Oh no," someone had said. "We will have to live with a monk." "How old is he?" someone else had asked. We teased a fellow Japanese female student saying, "Aha … get ready to cook for a monk." She thought we were serious. Later we had a good laugh. Gensho cooked for himself and often for the rest of us. We cooked for each other as we shared our responsibilities for a community kitchen. It was his smile that was so infectious. You could not be around him for more than a few moments and keep from laughing. Upon his arrival the atmosphere at

Blaisdell House changed. We respected him, and he treated us as friends. He turned out to be only ten years older than us. We learned that the arrangements for his being with us were made through the efforts of Professor Peggy Dornish of Pomona College. He was eager to learn everything about the American culture, and to improve his English conversation. We took it upon ourselves to introduce him to various positive aspects of the American culture. After all, we joked, we were a part of the Institute of World Religions and Cultures.

In 1973 I did not know that, in Japan, Gensho had already been selected to be a Zen master and to become a successor to his Zen master, Roshi Shibayama—a secret, well-guarded, that he kept to himself. I often wonder, had I known that he was such a highly respected monk, would my behavior toward him have been different? Would I have introduced him to pizza and James Bond movies at drive-in theatres? Perhaps not. In retrospect I am glad that I did not know. It allowed both of us to be "free." Since we shared rooms next to each other, gradually we became friends. As a graduate student specializing in Eastern Religions, I was taking courses in Buddhism and Zen. I was thrilled that I had Gensho to explain Zen to me. The Institute asked me to assist him as Gensho held *zazen* (sitting Zen meditation) sessions at Blaisdell House for students and the community. My job was to prepare the meditation room, welcome guests, provide them with cushions, and explain the basic routine of the evening. I proudly wore my *yukata* (Japanese kimono for men), which I had received as a gift from my Japanese roommate when I was an exchange student at the International Christian University in Tokyo in 1962. I enjoyed my job and began practicing Zen meditation. Gensho would gently correct my posture and teach me how to breathe. He spared me the Zen "stick."

I had been introduced to Zen Buddhism when I studied in Japan for a year, and had visited some of the famous Zen temples in Kyoto. I had gone to Tofukuji, but I did not remember visiting there. Now I was learning about Zen through everyday-living with a Zen monk, chosen to become a Zen master. As we interacted on a daily basis, Gensho's Zen life became manifest bit by bit. As a part of his daily routine, he could be observed every morning with a white handkerchief tied to his head, sweeping and cleaning the grounds around Blaisdell House. What I would consider a mundane chore, was a source of enjoyment for him. While the neighborhood slept, Gensho swept. Once I asked him about his unfailing dedication to pruning the bushes, sweeping the grounds, and picking up the dead leaves. He paused and, leaning on the rake with a smile on his face, answered, "Sweeping is a form of meditation. You know we have many stories in the Zen tradition where a monk received enlightenment while working in the garden. When he hit a rock in a certain way or broke a twig accidentally.... one monk even killed a snake and was awakened." Of course, I had read these stories in books. "Ah ... so you are trying to get enlightened, are you?" I talked back. He responded with laughter, but avoided my smart remark. "Work is meditation," he continued, "because Zen teaches to be in the present. Whatever you do you have to be in the here and now, be in the moment." I recalled what the professor had said in Buddhism class. We are bored when we do our chores. We want to hurry through them and by doing that we miss the present moment. Zen wants one to experience the "moment."

We frequently visited various pizza places in the neighboring towns around Claremont. Since Gensho routinely wore his monk's robe and shaved his head, wherever we went people were curious. He would greet them with a big smile. Over pizza he would share various *koans* (Zen questions) with us and have us brood over answers. Of course our answers were always wrong because we treated the *koans* as riddles. He would explain that in Zen the answer to a *koan* does not come through a rational mind. "Rationality has to be exhausted to open the intuitive mind," he would say. I found these conversations most interesting. I recalled what D. T. Suzuki had written: that the *koan* is to be nourished in those recesses of the mind where the rational mind cannot reach.[1] Gensho would relate his own experiences of struggling with *koan* studies at Nanzenji, where he trained under Roshi Shibayama. We found all that quite intriguing, but at the same time none of us really understood the full import of it for Zen. I remember how we puzzled over the well-known *koan*, "the sound of one hand clapping." We sat there brooding over the answer while our pizzas got cold. In the meantime Gensho chuckled and kept digging into the pizza. At one point, with a big smile on his face, he held up one hand in the air and started making clapping sounds with his fingers and palm joining together at a rapid rate, while holding the pizza slice in the other hand. As we listened to the sound of his one hand he said, "The answer is not that." We all had a big laugh. I had a keen desire to experience *koan* study—a dream which would not come true until 2001 when I made a second visit to Gensho's monastery in Kyoto.

At Claremont during my numerous discussions with Gensho, the issue of the existence of God would often come up. "Where is God?" he would ask me. As a seminary graduate who had also done postgraduate study in theology, I would quote Barth, Tillich, Teilhard, Radhakrishnan, Bonhoeffer, and others. We would tinker with Tillich's "ground of being," "ultimate concern," "God beyond God." etc. We would reflect on Radhakrishnan's Nirguna Brahman and Saguna Brahman. We would ponder over Buddha's silence on the question of God, the eternality of the world, and the questions of "non-edification." However, we would arrive at no decisive solution. Frustrated, I would say, "The issue of God in Christianity is a matter of faith." I saw the limitations of our inter-faith dialogue, useful as it was.

One day something interesting happened that left a lasting impression on my mind. I was conversing with some friends in our living room when Gensho burst into the room with a big

---

[1] See D. T. Suzuki, *Zen Buddhism* (New York: Doubleday, 1956), ch. 6.

smile and blurted out, "Ishwar, God exists." He caught me by surprise. I was dumbfounded. What's with Gensho? I thought. "He exists in your mind," he said and kept on walking toward his room. We didn't speak about this incident for a long time. It was not until much later that I learned that Gensho had had a unique experience at a Catholic church. A Catholic nun in one of the graduate seminars had invited Gensho to attend a special service at a monastery. As he recalled, when they entered the chapel, the monks were chanting, which turned into singing and back to chanting. Their music, dedication, prayerful mood, and total absorption overwhelmed Gensho. He thought, "Ah ... their God exists in their minds as Buddha Nature exists in mine." After that experience we never discussed the problem of the existence of God.

While working as a youth director in a church in San Bernardino, I invited Gensho to give a talk to the congregation. The talk went well and many people appreciated the Zen insights. Some, however, did not. Gensho did not get upset, but patiently explained the Buddhist perspectives on "emptiness," "no-self," and "detachment." He expressed the need for an inter-faith dialogue and religious tolerance. He insisted that the Buddhist concepts should not be perceived as "Buddhist." Buddhism was a traditional designation, but the truths were universal and cut across all labels. "If an egotistical and selfish life is bad for a Buddhist, it is bad for a Christian too," he said. "If attachment to worldly things causes problems for a Buddhist, it does for a Christian as well. If craving is a weakness for a Buddhist, it is for a Christian also." "Do you think that Jesus was a Buddhist since some of his teachings resemble Buddhism?" one person asked. Laughing, Gensho responded, "Was he a Buddhist? I don't know, but he had an Eastern mind." I immediately recalled how Radhakrishnan, an eminent Indian philosopher, had called Jesus an "Eastern seer."[2]

[2] For similarities between the teachings of Jesus and Eastern thought, see S. Radhakrishnan, *Eastern Religions and Western Thought* (New York: Oxford University Press, 1939), ch. V.

In winter if it snowed in the mountains of southern California, it was an event. Sometimes Mt. Baldy near Claremont had snow and we loved to drive up there. Like pilgrims we would climb up following the ski lifts to touch the white stuff. Often there would be no snow there, but we would have a clear view of the Pomona Valley from the top. Sometimes we would see a thick layer of smog settled in the valley below while we stood above it. Gazing down below we would wonder how we could live and breathe in that pollution. We would linger at the mountaintop as long as we could to take in the fresh air and then descend with deep regret. On one such occasion when the snow was clearly visible on Mt. Baldy, I invited Gensho to drive up with me to spend some time there. As we stood at the base of the mountain, the scene was spectacular. Blue, sunny sky with scattered clouds and the snow peak with brown underbrush presented a picture postcard view. I turned to Gensho and said, "Did you bring your camera to take a picture?" He looked at me with his usual captivating smile and said, "Ishwar-san, I am the mountain. I don't need to take the picture." He laughed, and I remained silent. This was an occasion for me to learn a bit more about Zen. Zen upholds the ideal of "one in all, all in one." It sees the inter-connectedness of all reality. One of the deepest insights of Zen is that we are all part of the One. This insight has far-reaching consequences for Zen life. I received a lesson in Zen from Gensho that day on Mt. Baldy.

Blaisdell House normally had rooms for five students who were Blaisdell fellows. The women lived upstairs and men downstairs. We shared a common kitchen and a common living room space with comfortable sofas and a black-and-white television set. We took turns cooking for the entire house and also shared the cleaning chores. Gensho became a member of the Blaisdell family. He took on all of the responsibilities and performed them with joy. I was astonished at his dedication and commitment to the Blaisdell family. Like any other family, we sometimes had problems. There were personality conflicts, lack of discipline in fulfilling our duties, and disagreements over menus. We all looked to Gensho as an arbitrator. We felt that he would have a discerning eye and determine right from wrong. I remembered how it bothered me that he was never judgmental. Even when in our discussions it was clear who was at fault, he would never condemn the guilty or expect a change of conduct. Although it was disturbing to me, it was years later that I understood the reasons for his behavior. By his own admission, he was rising beyond all "dualism." According to Zen, the average person lives with dualistic understanding created through the rational mind. This mind attaches to the "right" and "wrong" only to perpetuate more suffering. A Zen person transcends dualism, knows detachment, controls the ego, and exercises compassion. Through his behavior, Gensho was giving us a lesson in Zen.

Gensho's sense of humor kept us all amused. Students loved his company and he enjoyed interacting with everyone. Whether it was shopping for groceries or going to a restaurant, he attracted people. Some were curious about his looks—his shaven head and black robe—others wanted to ask about Zen. There is one incident that Roshi Keido Fukushima and I still chuckle about. One afternoon several of us had gone to visit a friend in a hospital. While waiting in the lobby, we encountered a robust middle-aged man who entered, looked at Gensho, and without pausing, shouted with glee, "Hey, where are you wrestling tonight?" "In Los Angeles, come and see me," came the instant reply from Gensho. "Okay, I'll be there," responded the man, as he kept walking. We burst into laughter, and had to leave the lobby. Instances like this were common occurrences with Gensho. At that time I did not know much about Zen and humor. Gensho admitted that before he entered into a Zen life, his personality was different. Much of his sense of humor developed during his life as a Zen monk. During his year in Claremont, he once visited San Francisco, particularly those areas frequented by the "hippies." As he explained, "I wanted to see them and interact with them." He recalled that as he got out of the car, many hippies surrounded him. One of them shouted, "Are you a hippie too?" "I am the patriarch of the hippies," replied Gensho. An instant rapport was established and he told them about Zen Buddhism. I loved to listen to Gensho's experiences in America. We seldom talked about Japan, but America was very much on his mind. I did not know that his Zen master, Roshi Shibayama, was grooming him to be an advocate of Zen in America—a task he has undertaken with utmost seriousness.

* * *

After I said goodbye to Gensho at the Ontario Airport, we lost touch. I left Claremont in 1974 and began my teaching career at Rutgers University. Gensho returned to his monastery in Japan to continue his Zen practice. However, his friendship remained fresh in my mind. In my classes I never failed to narrate instances from his exemplary Zen life. I often thought that maybe someday I would have an opportunity to travel to Japan to visit Gensho in his monastery. The years went by; the opportunity never knocked at my door.

Suddenly, through friends in Claremont, I learned that Gensho, as we knew him, was now Keido Fukushima, and had been appointed the Zen master of Tofukuji in 1980. I welcomed the news with great delight, but still there was no hope of seeing or visiting him.

In 1981 I moved to Ohio and began teaching at the College of Wooster. In 1989, one of my students, who had written an honor's thesis as a part of Wooster's independent study program, expressed his keen desire to go to a Zen monastery in Japan to practice meditation. As we explored the possibilities for him, I decided to call one of my professors at Claremont Graduate School to get Gensho's address. As I spoke with Professor Dornish, to my amazement she said, "Gensho is here. You can speak to him. He is a Roshi now, you know." I was overjoyed, but nervous, elated but hesitant, excited but cautious. How was I to address a Roshi? Would he remember me? Would he be willing to receive my student at his monastery? How would I start a conversation? I pondered on these thoughts for a day. I called the Faculty Club in Claremont where he was staying. He was not in. I was relieved of my anxiety and left a message for him to call me. "If he cherished our friendship, he would call me," I rationalized. "And if he does not, that would be fine. No harm done," I thought.

In the midst of a very busy day with student conferences, meetings, and classes, the phone rang. The voice on the other end said, "This is Roshi's assistant. You knew him as Gensho. He is now known as Keido Fukushima. He would like to speak to you. Hold on please." My heart began to race as I waited for the Roshi to get on the phone. "Hello Ishwar! Long time, no see. This is your friend, Gensho. How are you?" came the enthusiastic voice. I tried to greet him in my broken Japanese. "Oh ... your Japanese is much better than my English," he said and laughed. There was an instant rapport. It felt like only yesterday we had said goodbye and now we were talking again. We chatted a bit and then I asked him if my student could visit his monastery. "Of course, please send him. And [Gensho often begins his sentences with 'and'], when are you coming to my monastery? Please come anytime," he insisted. We had a very pleasant reunion on the phone. But he was in California and I was in Ohio. The chances of meeting were very slim. We never did meet. However I felt good about our telephone conversation. He sounded just the same and had not lost his sense of humor.

As it turned out, neither my student nor I made it to Gensho's monastery. Occasionally Gensho and I exchanged Christmas and New Year's greetings, but gradually we began to lose touch once again. Almost a decade passed and my dream to go to Japan remained unfulfilled. In 1998 I decided to teach a course in "Zen and the Arts in Japanese Culture." It became crucial that I visit Japan. I was fortunate to receive a travel grant from Earlham College's Japan study program, supplemented with a summer fellowship from the Faculty Development Fund at the College of Wooster. I called Gensho and asked permission to stay at Tofukuji for five weeks. He was more than pleased to extend his welcome. I was excited. I was about to return to Japan after thirty-six years of absence. I had spent the academic year of 1962-63 in Tokyo when Japan had emerged as an industrial nation from post World War II. The images of Nara and Kyoto began to flash in my mind as I entertained the thought of visiting those ancient cities again. I was to share in the life of the monastery—that is all I knew. I had no idea as to what to expect besides doing *zazen*. Gensho had mentioned that I would have complete freedom to do things in the city of Kyoto and to travel as I wished.

The momentous occasion arrived when I landed at Osaka-Kansai airport in May of 1999. The immigration officer was surprised to learn that the Roshi of Tofukuji was waiting for me outside. She hurried me through. "Welcome to Japan" were his first words to me as we hugged (an American habit he had picked up). His two attendants—training monks—remained bowed with respect as we exchanged greetings. Gensho took my hand while the monks took my bags. Hand in hand we made our way to the airport garage where his driver, Kimura-san, pulled up with a car. The approximately two-hour ride to Kyoto passed quickly. We talked about Blaisdell House, Claremont, our common friends, and his being a Roshi. We recalled the days of 1973 when we shared rooms at Blaisdell House. He seemed joyous, full of energy, and enthusiastic. He looked somewhat older and commented that I had aged also.

As the car pulled into the Tofukuji compound, I had the first glimpse of the ancient monastery that had a long history behind it. Recognized as one of the national treasures of Japan, it was now under the care of Keido Fukushima.

As we sat in the room where the Zen master entertained guests, he insisted that I should spend at least three days in a hotel before entering the *sodo* (monk's quarters). I knew that Japan was expensive and the hotel where he wanted me to go was rated among one of the best. I hesitated. "Don't worry, it is my hotel. Please stay freely." It seemed I had no choice. After some Japanese tea and refreshment, I was transported to the hotel near the Kyoto Railway Station. I was instructed to charge everything to my room, and to make sure that I had a meal at the revolving restaurant at the top of the hotel. I did. The view was breathtaking. During the three days, I traveled around Kyoto, re-learned to ride the subway, and got reacquainted with Japanese food. The jetlag limited my movement, but it did not deter me from roaming the streets of Kyoto. The Kyoto of 1962, which I remembered, was very different. Then there were street-cars, unpaved roads, and old market places. None of that was to be seen now. The present transportation system was ultra-modern. The streets were filled with buses, taxis, and cars. I had a culture shock.

Tofukuji, located not too far from the Kyoto Central Railway Station, is an enormous complex. Famous for its historic buildings, meditation halls, a bridge, Zen gardens and maple trees, it attracts tourists from all over Japan all year-round. I was given a room in the *sodo* (monks' quarters) area next to the *zendo* (meditation hall). The room was modest but comfortable. The head monk lived on one side of me and a monk from Thailand on the other side. The rest of the monks slept in the *zendo*, where they also studied and practiced *zazen*. From the very beginning I decided to follow the schedule of the monastery. It meant getting up at 3:00 a.m., meditating in the *zendo*, participating in the chanting, eating with the monks, practicing evening meditation, and going to bed around 10:30 p.m. when everyone slept. The first few days were difficult. It seemed that as soon as you had turned in for the night, the morning bell rang and the routine began all over again. My decision to follow the monks' schedule surprised the Roshi, but he did not object. I told him that I wanted to experience the Zen life, and he encouraged me to do that. During the day I was free to visit many temples and shrines in Kyoto and Nara. With the help of the Thai monk, whom we called Thana-san, I discovered Kyoto International Community House, where I began taking lessons in *sumiye* (painting) and *ikebana* (flower arrangement). I returned to this center in 2001 to take further lessons in the tea ceremony and Noh play. This was all in preparation for my "Zen and the Arts" class at the College of Wooster.

Living at the monastery provided an opportunity to fully participate in the monastic life. However, I did not go on the daily "begging" rounds and was not permitted to commence a *koan* study with the Zen master. I was told that if I were to return to Tofukuji some other time, I could take part in *dokusan* (*koan* interview with the master). I was disappointed, but made a resolution to return again to experience first-hand what I had read in books about *koan* study.

The best and most difficult part was participation in the sitting meditation. I was averaging five to six hours a day in *zazen* practice in the *zendo*. Soon after my arrival at *sodo*, I kept receiving messages from the Roshi to come to "night sitting." The night sitting was called a "free" sitting without being monitored by a *jikijitsu* (the carrier of the Zen stick). It was done on the veranda of the chanting hall overlooking a sand garden. Due to my jetlag I was falling asleep around 9:00 p.m. when the night sitting was about to commence. The messages from the Roshi, whom I had not seen for a few days, kept coming. I kept sending the message back that I fully intended to participate as soon as I was able to get over my jetlag. I don't know if the messages ever got to him since the head monk spoke very little English, and I was doubtful whether he understood what jetlag was.

The night meditation at Tofukuji is an experience never to be forgotten. At 9:00 p.m. in the *zendo*, the monks participate in a ritual which may appear ridiculous to visitors. At the sound of a bell, the meditation ends and the monks quickly bring out their mattresses and pretend to go to sleep. The *jikijitsu*, with his *keishaku* (Zen stick), makes a quick round, checks the lying positions, the neatness of the covers, smacks the slackers with his stick, and the lights are turned off. No sooner than the lights are out, the monks roll up their mattresses and rush out running for the night meditation which is held in another building. The visitors follow quietly, but quickly. On the fourth night of my stay at *sodo,* I decided to go for the night sitting. As visitors, Thana-san and I made our way through the dark corridors and walkways until we came to a closed sliding door at the chanting hall. From the other side a monk opened the door, which was our signal to enter the veranda and find a place at the end of the row where the monks were taking their positions. The first glimpse of the sand garden overlooking a hillock full of trees and flowering bushes was breathtaking. A pond separated the sand garden and the flower bushes. The entire complex was glistening in the summer moonlight. No wonder I was being encouraged to participate in this so-called "night sitting." The free meditation lasted for an hour. The visitors could leave early if they wished. After the first encounter, I seldom missed the night meditation. In fact, my first experience, which I interpreted to be a Zen experience, occurred here. Later the Zen master dismissed it as an experience produced by my "rational mind."[3]

In the *zendo, zazen* was difficult but manageable. I was permitted to take breaks as I felt it necessary. In the beginning I could sit only for twenty minutes at a stretch without needing a break. Gradually I got up to forty-five minutes. My shoulders, back, and legs ached. The head monk warned me not to overdo it and to take frequent breaks. For me the most difficult aspect to deal with in the meditation sessions was the slapping of the monks with the Zen stick. The visitors never got hit unless they requested to receive the stick, so I was safe. During my first stay at the monastery I never requested the stick. However the monks got hit whether they requested it or not. The new monks (first year trainees) often got hit as they dozed off. I had to reconcile myself with the fact that I was staying at a training

---

[3] Once during the night sitting meditation I began getting extremely clear pictures of Zen art. For example, a Zen person fishing with a big smile, but he has no hook attached to his line (I called it Zen fishing), or a Zen person golfing, but for the golf ball he had his head on the tee (I called it Zen golfing), or a Zen person playing cards, but his cards are blank (I called it Zen poker). The Zen master found these interesting but dismissed them as creations of my rational mind.

monastery where "discipline" was one of the cardinal rules. It was explained to me that receiving the Zen stick was considered an honor. When I spoke with the young training monks, they did not seem to mind receiving the stick. They accepted it as part of their training.

The stick got louder during the *sesshin* (week of intensive meditation). The Roshi suggested that I should participate in the *sesshin*. I eagerly agreed. During the *sesshin* long hours were spent in the *zendo*. For a week I committed myself not to go out of the monastery compound except for a half-hour walk in the evening. During the *sesshin*, the *jikijitsu* got to work. Almost every monk got hit; the new monks more often than others. I often took refuge in my room because I did not understand the significance of this ritual. I made several entries in my diary about my feelings on the Zen stick. I even took up this issue with the Roshi, which for me was an "abusive behavior" on the part of the *jikijitsu*. I thought that the Roshi was not aware of what went on in the *zendo* since his living quarters were at a distance, and he never came to the *sodo*. To my surprise, the Roshi knew every detail of the *sesshin* sessions. He defended the Zen stick. It was not until two years later that I truly grasped the meaning of "hitting" after a lengthy conversation with Keido.

During my five-week stay at Tofukuji, I had many opportunities to observe the behavior of the monks and the Zen master. I participated in many monastery rituals and attended several formal dinners with visiting guests and priests. Sometimes the Roshi would invite me to have a meal with him. I seized this opportunity to ask many questions and to tape our conversations. When I learned that Keido was making yearly trips to the United States, I asked him to come to the College of Wooster for a series of lectures and calligraphy demonstrations. He accepted the invitation. I later learned that, in Japan, Keido Fukushima was recognized as one of the best calligraphers. He had many pending orders for his work throughout Japan. Many of his works go to hundreds of sub-temples of the Tofukuji sect in the Rinzai school of Zen. He is also in demand for public speaking and constantly leaves the monastery to give speeches. He heads the board of Tofukuji priests and is involved in settling many disputes. Besides lecturing in the United States at various colleges and universities for two to three months every year, he also visits China where he is involved in a restoration project to rebuild an ancient temple and monastery. The more I talked with him, the more intriguing his life became for me.

It was during his second visit to the College of Wooster, in the spring of 2001, that I proposed to him that I wanted to write his biography. He hesitated, but I convinced him that the biography would focus on understanding Zen through the life of a Zen master. Furthermore, it would be useful for the college students who have a growing interest in Zen. I tried to convince him that his dream to establish an "international Zen" needed to be shared. Not only that, but his experiences in the West and his efforts to revive Zen in China needed a wider audience. He agreed, and this project was born. As we talked, he said, "You know that means that you would have to return to my monastery for a longer period of time." I agreed and began planning for my next visit. During my study leave from the College of Wooster in the fall of 2001, I spent three months at Tofukuji, gathering more material for the biography and learning more about Zen and the Arts. We met again in 2003 in Ohio and Japan.

My second stay at Tofukuji was more remarkable than the first one in 1999. Several senior monks had become priests and had left the monastery. Several junior monks now enjoyed senior status. There were also a few newcomers. I was given the same room, and the freedom to study Zen and the arts as I saw fit. I found my way back to the Kyoto International Community House, got reacquainted with some old teachers, and found some new ones. I became a bit more skillful in *sumiye* and *ikebana*, but Noh dancing remained demanding. The Noh teachers did not speak any English. Some fellow students tried to help, but in vain. The tea ceremony went well. I learned enough to be able to explain the fundamentals of the tea ceremony to my students in Wooster.

The most remarkable experience was to be able to do the *koan* study with Keido. Recognizing that my interest was genuine, he accepted me as one of his students. The *koan* that I was assigned was "Joshu's *mu*—Does a dog have the Buddha nature?"[4] I had read enough about the *koan* study to know that it would be a frustrating experience. The Zen master showed patience with me. However, for me, our relationship had changed. He was now my guru, and I his disciple. During *dokusan*, I found him to be serious, stern, and unapproachable. Often I was dismissed as soon as I opened my mouth to give my answer. Days went by before I began to be comfortable with my new relationship with him. Sometimes I thought he was going to hit me with his *nyoi* (a small stick the master carries) to awaken me to a new insight. He never did. During our interview it was my tendency to sit away from him. One evening he demanded, "Ishwar, come closer." I was certain that my day had come to be hit. It did not happen. I was relieved. Sometimes during our private moments at his visitor's room, the Roshi would ask, "So, how do you like the *koan* study?"

"It is hard, and I am scared of you," I would reply.

He would laugh and remark, "Oh! I am enjoying it."

"Good," I thought, "He has not lost his sense of humor." In moments like those, I was with Gensho again.

During my stay at *sodo*, although I was given the freedom to follow my own schedule, and stay "freely" as the master put it, I chose to follow the monastery schedule. It meant getting up at 3:00 a.m. and following the daily routine, which ended with the night sitting at 10:00 p.m. I intensified my *zazen* efforts in the *zendo*, trying to sit for an hour at a stretch. I failed. The most I could endure was forty-five minutes. I made a resolution that my Zen practice would be incomplete until I began receiving the Zen stick. During one meditation session I mustered enough

---

[4] In the *koan* called "Joshu's *mu*", the import of the *koan* is in how the Zen master Joshu uttered "*mu*" when he was asked, "Does a dog have Buddha nature?" The issue is, what about your "*mu*"?

courage and bowed to receive the stick. It hurt a little, but by the end of the session I did not feel any pain. Gradually I began requesting the stick more often, and it felt quite normal. Another *sesshin* week came, and the training intensified. This time I was not disturbed over the fact that the monks were getting hit. I had a deeper understanding of how the *jikijitsu* and the monks worked as a team. Together they had the same goal to mature in their training. On one occasion I found a junior monk, who was being hit the most (because he was consistently falling asleep during *zazen*), thanking the *jikijitsu* for encouraging him. Although I was being hit rather gently (I was the oldest person in the *zendo*), I discovered that the sting of the stick kept me awake. One night at about 1:00 a.m., I awoke with an excruciating pain in my left leg. I thought a centipede had bitten me (I had seen one crawling near my mattress earlier). I went to a hospital, but the x-ray showed no damage to the toes. Practicing *zazen* sitting in one position caused the pain. I was advised to frequently change the position. After awhile the pain went away.

I had come to Tofukuji to practice *zazen*, to study *koan*, but primarily to do extensive interviewing of Roshi Keido Fukushima. My study of the Zen arts was going well in town. However the Roshi could not find time to sit with me for any length of time. His schedule was extremely tight. Sensing my anxiety, he made changes in his schedule and started granting me extensive interviews. I made approximately sixteen hours of audiotapes with him before I left Japan. During his visit to the College of Wooster, our conversation continued. Thanks to the internet which facilitated further inquiries via e-mail. What follows in these pages is a remarkable story of a living Zen master.

The Making

of the

Zen Master

The Kyo-zo at Tofukuji which houses the Buddhist Sutras

Born as Ken'ichi to the Fukushima family in 1933, Gensho spent his early childhood in Kobe City, Japan. As his parents were divorced, he spent his childhood with his grandparents. Grandmother Hisa was a devout Buddhist and a loving parent. She would have a lasting influence on Ken'ichi's life. She respected Kukai, the founder of the Shingon Buddhist sect, and would take her grandson to Mt. Koya several times.[1] Recalling those days, Gensho remarks, "Due to my grandmother, I naturally gained a fundamental knowledge of Buddhism. As a child I grew up praying at the *Butsu-dan* (Buddha altar) at home and making the water offerings to the Buddha." During his kindergarten years he also came in contact with the new religion of Tenri Kyo.[2] He saw no difference between Buddhism and Tenri Kyo, but was attached to the "religious feelings" that they provided. Although his parents divorced, he kept in touch with his mother, Chiyoko, who had moved to Tokyo and remarried. He recalls: "My mother's family were strong believers in the teachings of the Zen master Dogen. I made a few trips to the famous temple of Eiheiji as well."[3] It is

---

[1] Kukai, also known as Kobo Daishi (774 - 835 C.E.), elected Mt. Koya as a site for his monastery-temple after his return from China. His school (Shingon), known as the esoteric school of Buddhism in Japan, emphasizes the mysticism associated with the body, speech, and mind of Mahavairochana (the great Sun Buddha).

[2] Regarded as one of the newer religions of Japan, Tenri Kyo came into existence in 1838. It claims that God the Parent, Tenri-o-no-Mikoto became revealed through Oyasama, Miki Nakayama to save all humankind. It claims to have a worldwide following.

[3] Eiheiji, the "temple of eternal peace," is one of Soto Zen's two head temples, and is located deep in the mountains near the rugged west coast of Japan close to Fukui City. It was founded by Dogen Zenji (1200 - 1253 C.E.).

noteworthy that Ken'ichi (destined to be a Zen master) was exposed to a variety of forms of Buddhism in Japan at an early age.

Ken'ichi's grandfather wanted him to become a lawyer. The grandfather was annoyed at his son, who had promised to become a lawyer, but secretly got involved in the trading business and lost all of the family fortune. The grandfather, who was blind, made his son divorce Ken'ichi's mother out of anger. He eventually disowned his son and began grooming his grandson to become a lawyer. However, it was the grandmother's influence that won out. Remembering his early childhood, Roshi Fukushima ponders: "My blind grandfather made a fortune, his son wasted it, and I became a monk. There must be a reason behind it all." One of the reasons was his love and respect for his grandmother. He grew very close to her. She transmitted her faith to Ken'ichi. When he was in the 2nd grade, the grandmother made sure that he went to a temple elementary school. There he was taught the art of *shu-ji* (writing). He recalls how his grandmother insisted that he should bring his writing samples home so she could check them. Ken'ichi, with his child wisdom, had one of his friends do the writing samples for him. The grandmother knew that it was not Ken'ichi's work and scolded him. Gensho admits that he hated to go to the elementary school, but gradually began to enjoy it. By the time he became a 5th grader, he could not wait to go to the temple to practice *shu-ji*. He won an award for his writing abilities, and his was the only work selected for a display at the temple shrine. He comments: "Today I have pretty good handwriting [he is famous for his calligraphy] because of the work I did in my childhood, and I am very thankful for my grandmother's strict education."

When Ken'ichi entered the 6th grade, World War II broke out. This was a difficult time for Japanese people, especially the children. To protect them, the government had a plan to evacuate many children from Kobe City. About eighty boys and girls were sent to Hofukuji, a Zen training monastery in Okayama prefecture. Ken'ichi was one of them. To my amazement, when he recalls the war, he laughs. "As kids, as we saw the American planes hovering over Kobe City, we would shout, 'kill the Americans,' and run out on the streets. I was angry and wanted to join the military," he remembers. He becomes sad and remarks: "Many of my friends went to war and died." He did not like being separated from his sister and his grandmother.

On March 13, 1945, the first bombing of Kobe City took place. On July 5th, during the second bombing, his home was destroyed. He recalls: "The day of the second bombing, I was at home in Kobe. Since my father was not home, my grandmother had to escape with me and my sister in the rain of bombs." He describes the scene with a vivid description of chaos, people dying, homeless wandering the streets, and the lost searching for loved ones.

Michi, Ken'ichi's sister, was seriously ill during the bombing raids. However, she had to move in order to survive. He recalls: "My sister said that she would rather die at home, but my grandmother carried her all the way until we reached a safe place. At the evacuation site, our meals consisted of rice balls with some corn in it. My sister had typhoid and this food was not good for her." Gensho remembers his sister with fond memories. She was interested in foreign languages and tried to learn English and German. He regrets that during the end of her life he could not be with her. He had to return to Hofukuji. His grandmother objected, but gave him permission since the train fare had been excused for the war victims. "When I left, my sister was sleeping so I did not want to disturb her," he recalls. When she did awake, she called for him and asked her grandmother not to let him go. The grandmother rushed to the railway station, but Ken'ichi was lost in the crowd, not to be found. On June 13, 1945, Michi died at the age of sixteen. Ken'ichi did not learn of her passing away for several days. When he told his fellow students about the bombing of Kobe City, many of them cried for losing their homes. A few days later, upon his return to

Hofukuji, a school teacher from Kobe visited the temple and informed Ken'ichi of his sister's death. He remembers: "I went to a nearby hill and cried for a whole day."

Soon after hearing of his sister's death, Ken'ichi fell ill. His patron at Hofukuji, Roshi Okada, immediately had him admitted to a hospital. Ken'ichi had been infected with typhoid. The grandmother visited Hofukuji to take care of him. He soon recovered. It was at this time that Roshi Okada asked the grandmother to leave Ken'ichi under his care. She declined, stating that she had to fulfill her husband's promise and educate Ken'ichi to become a lawyer. Ken'ichi also agreed. On August 15, 1945, the war ended. Gensho reflects: "We listened to the news of the ending of the war at a nearby police station. Everyone there was crying." After the war, life was miserable. The family had to survive on sweet potatoes. In 1947, both Ken'ichi and his grandmother fell seriously ill. He recovered, but the condition of his grandmother worsened. The doctor gave her an injection but her weak body could not withstand it. Gensho remembers: "Her death was more shocking to me than my sister's. I think after the bombing of Kobe she was completely worn out. Then, after my sister died, surviving the war was too much for her. She was only fifty-six years old."

The death of his grandmother had a traumatic effect on the young Ken'ichi's life. He couldn't understand why the members of his family, to whom he was so close, died. First it was his grandfather, then his sister, and now his grandmother. From this time onward he began to contemplate on becoming a monk. He recalls how his Chinese writing teacher was instructing Buddhist teachings through writing. She had once said, "If one person becomes a monk, then his entire family will go to heaven for the ninth generation." Gensho remembers how he made the decision to enter a monastery. "After the death of my grandmother, I suddenly remembered what the teacher had taught us, and I decided to become a monk to appease the souls of my sister and grandmother." His mother did not favor his becoming a monk, but his stepfather thought that it was a good idea.

Which monastery should he enter? That was a difficult question. Since his grandmother had followed the Shingon sect, he thought he should go to Mt. Koya and enter the monastery there. He bought a ticket for Mt. Koya but, before boarding the train, he thought, "I should consult my mentor Okada-san at Hofukuji before I make this decision." He exchanged his ticket for Okayama and headed in that direction. Little did he know that this decision was to change his life forever. The lawyer-to-be was about to enter a Zen monastery as a monk.

Priest Okada was now Roshi Okada. Sensing Ken'ichi's dilemma, the Roshi advised him to stay at Hofukuji and begin the Zen training as a young monk under him. Recalling his entry into Hofukuji, Gensho recalls, "Since Okada-sensei had been so kind to me, and he was gentle with his students, I decided to become his disciple." Roshi Okada put one condition in front of Ken'ichi. Upon entering the monastery, he would have to cut off all family ties. Ken'ichi agreed and paid a visit to his mother, who proudly gave her permission for him to go ahead with his decision. He also visited many relatives in Osaka since he was instructed to leave them behind. He resolved to enter the monastery on Japan's Constitution Day—May 3rd. The year was 1946.

With great excitement and anticipation, Ken'ichi presented himself at Hofukuji. He still remembers that as he made his way through the monastery corridors, someone shouted, "Who goes there? Walk quietly." As he entered Roshi Okada's room, he heard the Roshi say, "You fool, bow before you enter the room." Ken'ichi slightly bent his head in courtesy, but was rebuked again. He was shocked to observe that the kind and gentle priest, Okada, was so stern and strict as a Zen master. He realized that his relationship with Okada was now that of a master and disciple. His first lesson at the monastery had started. In retrospect, he now realizes that Roshi Okada's behavior was just right. New monks at the monastery must adapt to a strict and disciplined life. "Zen training is meant for those who are willing to endure the hardship of the monastic life. It is not meant to

Roshi Okada

be an easygoing and relaxed life. The experience requires detachment from layman's life," he reflects. As a young monk, he was named Genko, but Roshi Okada later changed it to Gensho. Pleased with his new name, Gensho began his monastic training. He was only thirteen years old.

Gensho became a member of the community of "five little monks." The life was difficult. It was not getting up in the early morning that was so hard; rather, it was the cold. During the winter season the monastery had no heat. The room where the monks lived was freezing cold. Since the young monks' quarters were next to Roshi Okada's room, they could not complain or make noise. Silently they endured every hardship. Gensho befriended Esho, another monk who was a year older than him. Together they decided to share the same bed to keep warm. However, after some time, Esho escaped the monastery when the Roshi was away. He could not completely embrace the monastic life. During the first winter, Gensho suffered from frostbite. He recalls: "Our *sutra* reading started at 9:00 p.m. It was my job to signal the reading by hitting two wooden blocks together as clappers. One day as I hit the bars, the blood from my hands splashed on my face." At moments like this, Roshi Okada tried to encourage the young monks. He said that the first three years were difficult, but that it would get better. Once Gensho responded, "Does that mean that if I waited for four years it would be warmer in the winter and cooler in the summer?" Sometimes he cried, when alone, over his fate in the monastery. He thought to himself, "I should have gone to Mt. Koya. Perhaps the life would have been easier there." Little did he know that due to the higher elevation, Mt. Koya was much colder than Hofukuji. There was some wisdom in Roshi Okada's suggestion that things would improve. Gensho remarks, "By the end of the third year the life at the monastery was no longer painful. My body became conditioned and I got used to the rhythm of the monastic life. I was grateful to Roshi Okada that he encouraged us to stay on. I gained confidence in becoming a monk."

Once Roshi Okada had to remove some old paintings from a room for public display. He asked Gensho to handle these with care since they were national treasures. For the first time Gensho looked at Sesshu's paintings, who had been a monk at Hofukuji.[4] He thought to himself, "I can do that." Now he laughs at his childish comment. He states, "Only after I became a Zen master did I realize that Sesshu had done those paintings in his 'Zen mind.' I can now appreciate his genius as a Zen master who expressed his Zen experience through art." Today Roshi Keido Fukushima is an accomplished calligrapher who expresses his "Zen mind" through his extraordinary brush work. A few examples of his work are presented in this book.

Roshi Okada was a strict disciplinarian. He would often punish the young monks by hitting and kicking them when they made some mistakes. Gensho recalls that the Roshi would line them up and begin his striking with the oldest monk. However he would stop by the time he came to the third monk. Since Gensho was at the end of the line, he would be spared. After many years, when Roshi Okada was in his advanced age and had mellowed, Gensho paid him a visit and asked him, "Roshi Okada, why did you stop your spanking by the third monk and never made it to the end of the line?" He remembers that Roshi Okada laughed and told him that by the time he struck the third monk, the rest of them were trembling with fear, so he did not need to hit them. Both had a hearty laugh on recalling this incident. Now he feels that Roshi Okada's strictness was very good for the training monks. For Gensho, "He was truly a Zen master who believed in a disciplined life. His severe treatment was a form of love. It was out of his affection for all of us that he behaved that way. At the time I did not realize that, but now I do."

---

[4] Sesshu (1421-1506 C.E.), who trained at Hofukuji, is respected as one of the most famous artists of Japan. After his Zen master recognized his artistic genius, Sesshu was sent to China to further his studies. He is famous for his painting of a mouse. Sometimes, Hofukuji is referred to as "the temple of the mouse" because of Sesshu.

"Is that why you are so strict with your training monks at Tofukuji?" I asked.

He broke out with laughter and said, "Maybe. I don't know."

While training as a monk, Gensho continued his secular education at a local junior high school in Soja City. At school his teacher declared him a math genius because he could easily solve math problems by using trigonometric functions. Once, another student asked the teacher what was the cause of hiccups? The teacher could not answer, but Gensho offered the answer that it was due to the convulsions of the diaphragm. He got the reputation of being a "smart student." Gensho recalls, "Everyone thought that I was smart, but actually the educational standard at this school was very low." He enjoyed his high school years and was selected to give the Founder's Day speech for two years. The high school he attended had become co-ed and the female students treated him with respect. He attended the school during the daytime while living at the monastery. In high school the studies were demanding and there was a lot of homework to complete. However the monastery rule was that the lights were to be turned off and all monks should go to sleep at 9:00 p.m. Gensho, with another fellow monk (whom he called his brother monk) decided to use the altar candles for studying. However, the Roshi remembered the old and the new candles well. Gensho, with his brother monk, decided to use the old candles anyway, but to return them when they had melted about one centimeter. One day his fellow monk suggested that this arrangement was not working out well, and that they should collect some fireflies to produce light. So they collected about fifty fireflies near a stream and put them in tea bags. However the light was not enough. The next day they caught one hundred fireflies but still could not read the English dictionary because the "light" kept flashing. The other monk suggested that perhaps they should read the *sutras* instead since the letters there were much bigger than the dictionary's. The plan was successful. Recalling this incident Keido Fukushima remarks, "We studied the *sutra* until midnight, and that is one of the nicest memories of my student life." Once Roshi Okada caught Gensho studying secretly for high school exams under a dim light in a storage closet. The Roshi chided, "A monk does not have to study. Train your real ability rather than becoming number one in school." Gensho recalls, "That night I went to bed early, but thought to myself that it was far easier to study than to train as a monk."

The high school life came to a successful ending and Gensho started thinking about university. At high school his advisor advised him to study Buddhism at Tokyo University. However Roshi Okada seriously opposed this idea. He was afraid that if Gensho ended up at Tokyo, he would get involved in secular life and lose interest in becoming a Zen monk. Okada himself had studied at Tokyo and knew of the temptations it presented to young men. He reportedly said to Gensho, "No school in Tokyo. Students there really don't study but fool around." Thus it was decided that Gensho should study Buddhism at a university in Kyoto. Now he had to make a decision whether to go to Otani University or to Ryukoku. While struggling to make a decision, Gensho had a chance meeting with Roshi Shibayama who was visiting Roshi Okada at Hofukuji. They had been fellow students at Nanzenji, a well-known Zen training monastery in Kyoto.

Gensho knew that Roshi Okada had great respect for Shibayama. What he did not know was that in a few years he would become a disciple of Shibayama—a relationship that would last until Shibayama's death in 1974. He recalls how his first meeting with Roshi Shibayama left a lasting impression on him. Due to Roshi Okada's laudatory remarks about Shibayama, Gensho imagined him to be a very tall man with a robust personality. The day Shibayama was to visit Hofukuji, Gensho was instructed to wait for the arrival of the taxi that brought Shibayama, to open the door, and escort Shibayama to the temple gate. To his surprise, when he opened the taxi door, a tiny man stepped out and in a very soft voice said, "Thank you very much." Gensho was still looking for the famous Shibayama, not realizing that his master-to-be was speaking to him. He remembers: "When Shibayama Roshi saw my face, he gave me a truly warm greeting and a radiant smile. I will never forget that. During his stay at Hofukuji I was privileged to talk with him and he captured my heart. I decided to be a monk like him." When Shibayama learned about Gensho's dilemma about which university to choose, he recommended Otani in Kyoto.

At Otani, Gensho began an in-depth study of Indian Buddhism under the well-known scholar, Susumu Yamaguchi. Yamaguchi lectured on the Buddhist concepts of dependent co-origination (*paticcasamuppada*) and emptiness (*shunyata*).[5] Gensho realized that understanding these concepts was central to the understanding of Zen. Yamaguchi taught him more than a mere study of Buddhism. Since he was a scholar as well as a devout priest, his devotion to Buddhism made Gensho realize that "Zen was not only about enlightenment, but also about salvation."

As his studies in Buddhism proceeded, Gensho began contemplating graduate studies. However, to obtain a scholarship for graduate study was very difficult. One had to study very hard to qualify for educational funds. "To get the funds I studied like crazy, and as a result of that, luckily I was able to graduate with a top grade," states Gensho.

Roshi Okada had given his permission to Gensho to graduate from Otani on the condition that he would return to Hofukuji to continue his Zen training. Consequently the graduate school was out of the question. When he returned to Hofukuji with the idea to continue graduate work in Buddhism, he faced opposition from Roshi Okada. It led to a nightlong discussion in which Okada tried to convince Gensho to return to Hofukuji. However Gensho was determined to pursue graduate work. He remembers: "Finally at midnight, Roshi Okada asked

---

[5] According to the doctrine of *paticcasamuppada* (dependent co-origination), the process of life is explained through the chain of causation, at the root of which is "ignorance."

what I would do if he did not give me the permission. I simply told him that I would have to stop being his disciple. When Roshi Okada realized that I was ready to be expelled from the monastery, he gave his permission." Again, the condition was that Gensho would finish a master's course and return to Hofukuji.

At Otani, when Professor Yamaguchi realized that Gensho wanted to study Zen, he advised him to enter the Chinese Buddhist studies program. So he shifted from Indian Buddhism to Chinese Buddhism. For his master's thesis, Gensho focused on the *Lin Chi Records*. He spent an entire summer at Hofukuji, during the break from Otani, poring over the Rinzai papers (*Lin Chi Records*).

As he began writing his thesis, Roshi Okada fell ill and Gensho had to return to the monastery to nurse him. But that meant he lost time working on his thesis. He recalls: "I remembered about a famous Japanese scholar, Yukichi Fukuzawa, who did not have a fixed time to study. Whenever he felt sleepy he would lie down beside his desk, and whenever he woke up he would go back to studying. I thought I could do the same." So, inspired by Fukuzawa, Gensho closed all the windows of his room and buckled down to writing. He was able to make up for the lost time and finish his thesis.

While pursuing the course work for his Ph.D. degree, Gensho realized that something very important was lacking in his studies. It was the Zen "experience." Studying the Rinzai papers had reinforced this feeling. The feeling was so overwhelming that he quit his Ph.D. studies and entered Nanzenji in 1961. His guru was none other than Roshi Shibayama. Ultimately he would spend eleven years as a monk at this monastery.

Gensho looks at the Nanzenji years as some of the most crucial years in his Zen training. He was a twenty-eight year old scholar of Buddhism when he began his *koan* study with Roshi Shibayama. Recalling his encounter with *koan* studies, Gensho remarks, "I thought that since I was a scholar of Buddhism, *koan*

Roshi Shibayama

study would be easy for me. Furthermore I also thought that due to my graduate studies I was intellectually ahead of my fellow monks and was, after all, an expert on the *Lin Chi Records*." The first three years at Nanzenji were difficult for Gensho. The *koan* studies became increasingly frustrating. During *mondo*, Roshi Shibayama would sarcastically say to him that he should go back to the university and study more, implying that Gensho thought like a scholar not like a *koan* student. Gensho would often cite from the *Lin Chi Records* as he gave answers to his *koan*s. That would fail to impress Shibayama. He told Gensho, "Be a fool." Today, pondering over these years, Keido Fukushima laughs as he narrates his struggles with *koan* study. "How stupid I was," he says, "I thought I had to come up with a logical answer to the *koan*, so I applied my rational mind to the utmost, without any success." After awhile, he began asking his fellow students, "Did the Roshi tell you to 'be a fool'?" "No," they replied. "He asked us to 'study hard.'" Laughing, he continues, "That was the wisdom of Shibayama. He knew that I had to give up my knowledge while the others had to gain some more."

In his third year, Gensho decided to follow the advice of his master and become a fool. He stopped giving logical answers, and the Roshi stopped asking him to be a fool. Subsequently the fourth and fifth years went smoothly and Gensho completed his *koan* studies.

Roshi Keido Fukushima never tires of praising the two Zen masters under whom he had the opportunity to study. "I was fortunate to study under the two great Zen masters of Japan, Roshi Okada and Roshi Shibayama," he says. "Both have affected my personality." While Okada was a strict disciplinarian, Shibayama was gentle. Where Okada was funny, Shibayama was serious. Both were deeply concerned about their disciples and wanted to train them well in the Zen life. Gensho recalls how once at Hofukuji, Roshi Okada asked him how he liked Shibayama. Gensho responded that Shibayama was one level higher than Okada. When Okada inquired in what way, Gensho answered,

"Shibayama Roshi is so peaceful." "How about me?" asked Okada. "You make me nervous," came the reply from Gensho. At that Roshi Okada laughed loudly and remarked, "Well, I cannot compete with Shibayama Roshi." The conversation ended there. Okada had much respect for Shibayama.

At Nanzenji Gensho had many religious experiences, but one in particular was profound. It occurred sometime during the end of his third year during the winter intensive training session (*rohatsu*). He explains: "*Rohatsu*, a weeklong winter session, is known as 'monk killer.' During this period the entire week is perceived as one day. The monks are not allowed to sleep at all. Most of the time is spent in *zazen*." He knew that both Roshi Okada and Roshi Shibayama had their "awakening" as monks in the third year of their training during *rohatsu*. Gensho thought that he would be lucky if he got his "experience" during the fourth or fifth year of training. To his delight it occurred during his third year at Nanzenji. Was it a *satori* experience? I remember that once in Claremont, I had naively asked him, "Gensho, have you had a *satori* experience?" He replied then, "If you had asked me this question in Japan, I would have said no, but since you are asking me in America, I can say yes." Since I was interviewing him in Japan in 2001, I did not pursue this issue. At Tofukuji, the monks never discussed *satori*. Whenever I persisted in asking them about their *satori* experience, they responded with a hearty laugh. Thus, without asking him to label his experience, I did ask Gensho what a *satori* experience was like. He proceeded to tell me this incident. "At Nanzenji there is a small hill. I used to walk near there, look at it, and often smile at the high school students who walked by there as well. One day as I walked by, I looked at the hill and it was truly amazing. I was totally lost as if there was no 'me.' I stood gazing at the hill. Some students walked by and one of them said something like 'look at that crazy monk.' Finally I came out of it. Life was never the same for me. I was free." After this experience Gensho still had two more years of *koan* study.

As his fate would have it, Gensho was chosen by Roshi Shibayama to accompany him to the United States. At this time, he was the head monk at Nanzenji. Thus, in 1969, they came to Claremont Graduate School in Claremont, California. Claremont was the place where the famous Zen scholar, D. T. Suzuki, had taught Buddhism for a year and had established a friendly connection. Also, at the age of 90, when D. T. Suzuki decided to end his United States visits, he had recommended Roshi Shibayama to Columbia University as his successor. Thus began Shibayama's odyssey in the United States. In 1969, there were still professors at Claremont who were friends with D. T. Suzuki and wanted to invite Shibayama. That year, with the help of Gensho and Miss Kudo, an interpreter, they started sitting meditation sessions at Blaisdell House in Claremont. This was something Roshi Shibayama had longed to do but could not in previous years. Gensho was chosen to accompany Roshi Shibayama because it had been decided by Shibayama and Roshi Okada that Gensho would become a Zen master and succeed Okada at Hofukuji. By this time Gensho had completed his *koan* training and was pursuing his post-*koan* special training required of all Zen masters in Japan.

After his first United States tour, Gensho returned to Nanzenji and, in 1972, took the office of vice-resident priest of Hofukuji under Roshi Okada. Soon after his arrival at Hofukuji, Shibayama proposed to Okada that Gensho should return to the United States to continue the work that Shibayama had started. Roshi Shibayama was advancing in age and wanted a successor. While Roshi Okada was agreeable, Gensho declined. He recalls: "My reason for denying was my poor English. When I was at Claremont in 1969, I realized that I had no command of the English language. Furthermore, I thought that someday when I became the Zen master I would groom a disciple who might be suitable for America." When Gensho shared this thought with Roshi Shibayama, the Roshi retorted, "In that case we will have to wait for another generation before your disciple can go to the States. You have to go." Also, Gensho clearly remembers that Shibayama said, "If you do not like to speak bad English, then keep silent for a year and sit in meditation." Recalling this event, Gensho laughs and says, "It was a master's command to his disciple, so I decided to obey him. Also, I would not like to be silent and sit in meditation for a year."

In 1973, Claremont Graduate School invited Gensho for a year as a visiting scholar. He was given the freedom to sit in any of the classes, improve his English, and hold *zazen* sessions at the Blaisdell Institute. It became this writer's job to assist him. Thus started our lasting friendship.

Gensho remembers: "In 1974, President Alexander of Pomona College asked me to extend my stay at Claremont." However Gensho decided to return to Hofukuji. When I asked him why he did not extend his stay, he replied, "I loved Claremont very much. I had many good friends, including you, and everything was very comfortable. However I was getting too attached to Claremont. So I decided that I must leave." In 1974, when the residents of Blaisdell said goodbye to him at the Ontario Airport, Gensho was returning to Hofukuji to continue to assist Roshi Okada. That same year Roshi Shibayama asked him to go to Brazil, but Roshi Okada refused. During Gensho's absence from Hofukuji, his half-brother, who also became a Zen priest, was assisting Roshi Okada. In August 1974, Shibayama fell ill and died. Gensho grieved for him for a long time.

In 1975, Gensho had another offer to return to Claremont for yet another year to lecture and hold meditation sessions. He was torn between his love for Hofukuji on the one hand and Claremont Graduate School on the other. Since Claremont had been "so kind to him," as he put it, he wanted to return the favor. He was extremely touched by the faculty, students, and even little children in Claremont. He recalls: "Once I was shopping for groceries at a local market [he had duties to cook for Blaisdell House], and when I came out of the store I had two bags full of stuff. It was a long walk to Blaisdell House. I did not have a car, so I had to walk. A little boy with his bike approached me and wanted to help. When he realized my dilemma, he glad-ly said, 'Oh! I can help you.' He carried my bags. I will never forget his kindness to me." Gensho has many stories like this one when people in America extended their assistance to him. Therefore returning to America was natural for him. However he declined the offer to return to Claremont because Roshi Okada needed him at Hofukuji. Claremont's offer was repeated again and again, with a request for a shorter visit of three months. Gensho kept declining. He thought to himself, "Perhaps I can do much more for America after I become a Zen master."

While Gensho was busy at Hofukuji in Okayama, another drama was unfolding in Tofukuji in Kyoto. In 1979, the head abbot and Zen master of Tofukuji had died. Tofukuji was a well-known training monastery, as well as a national treasure. The council of priests from Tofukuji was looking for the head abbot's replacement. To find a replacement for Roshi Hayashi was not an easy task. In Rinzai Zen there are fourteen sects. Tofukuji is the main temple and the training monastery for the Tofukuji sect. It has twenty-five sub-temples and twenty-five resident priests. Whoever was to assume the responsibility would have to be a good administrator, a skillful head abbot, and a Zen master in order to train the monks. Since Hofukuji also belonged to the Rinzai sect, a team of priests visited Roshi Okada and requested that Gensho be sent to Tofukuji to be appointed as the new abbot. Roshi Okada refused because he wanted Gensho to succeed him one day. In 1979, the team visited Hofukuji six times, but was refused. Finally a head abbot who was older than Roshi Okada came with another team of priests to ask for Gensho. This time Roshi Okada realized that the matter was serious because the older abbot sat below Okada, repeatedly requesting for Gensho. Finally, recognizing the crisis situation at Tofukuji, Roshi Okada gave in. When the agreement was ritually finalized, Roshi Okada reportedly said, "I feel like my treasure was stolen from me." Recalling that event Roshi Keido Fukushima states, "I was very much touched by my master's deep love for me."

On October 10, 1980, Gensho came to Tofukuji in Kyoto as Roshi Keido Fukushima. He intended to return to Hofukuji periodically to help Roshi Okada but, as he recalls, Okada had said, "You should be determined to bury your bones at that temple." So he stayed at Tofukuji to start a new life. However, he made a bargain with Roshi Okada saying, "If I do not find any student monk within three years, I will come back to Hofukuji." Roshi Okada encouragingly replied, "Soon there will be many students since it is a very famous temple."

Upon his arrival Roshi Fukushima did not find any students, but three cats. He remembers how these cats sunbathed near his living quarters in the morning sun. He tried to gently chase them away, but they would not leave. He chides, "One of them looked at me so casually as if to say, why don't you leave, you are the newcomer? We have been living here for a long time." For the first three days the new Roshi was all alone at Tofukuji. According to the monastic discipline, he woke up at 3:00 a.m., chanted *sutra*s, cleaned the temple, and made tea for the guests. After three days one student showed up. Finally there were three monks during the first season and twelve by the second year. The cats left on their own. Tofukuji began to thrive as a training monastery.

Upon his arrival at Tofukuji, Keido became the 303rd resident priest. In the beginning people wondered if he would succeed as an administrator and the Zen master. He states: "I took my work seriously and wanted to make Tofukuji a successful monastery. So I worked hard. I kept postponing my trips to the United States because I was needed at home."

When China began to open up after the Cultural Revolution, Roshi Fukushima was invited to visit there and help rebuild an old Zen temple. In the beginning Fukushima was not eager to go to China due to his commitment at home. However in 1981, a delegation of thirty priests from the Tofukuji sect of Zen in Japan made a trip to southern China. Since Zen was introduced from China, Japan had maintained a connection with the motherland. Tofukuji had a special connection with

China because the first patriarch of Tofukuji, Shoichi (Ben'en, 1202-1280 C.E.), had spent six years studying under Buk-kan (1178-1249 C.E.) at Kin Zan temple in China. Finally he had been given a license by Buk-kan and returned to Japan to teach Zen at Tofukuji. He had brought back many stories, maps, and manuals of significance, which were placed at Tofukuji. During the Cultural Revolution, Kin Zan temple had been destroyed as many other centers of Buddhist worship were torn down. Keido states: "During the Sung dynasty this temple was the highest among the Rinzai sect. Many Zen masters from Japan, including Dogen (Soto), and the founder of the Obaku sect had visited there. Therefore all Japanese Zen sects looked up to Kin Zan Mountain as the original place of importance."

At first the delegate priests from Tofukuji could only visit Koshu City located below the Kin Zan Mountain. The Buddhist Association of Koshu City welcomed them, but they were told that since the Chinese Army had a camp in the Kin Zan Mountain, they could not visit there. In 1985, to their delight, they were permitted to climb the mountain to make a pilgrim-age, but only the priests of the Tofukuji sect could do so. Keido remembers: "There were thirty of us who climbed the rough ter-rain of the mountain which took us about an hour and a half. When we reached the top we discovered that the ground was flat. All the ancient temple buildings had been destroyed. Some Chinese farmers had been living there after the Cultural Revolution. It was an empty holy place. After seeing the site we all cried with joy and wanted to visit there every year." Eventually the Buddhist Association of Koshu City asked the Japanese delegation to help them rebuild the temple. All of the Rinzai sects began helping, but Tofukuji took the lead. Roshi Keido Fukushima was selected to head the rebuilding project. The Roshi recalls: "This was an historical moment for us. I glad-ly took up the challenge of becoming part of an important his-tory. Since at Tofukuji we had Shoichi's records that he had brought back from Kin Zan, we showed them to the Buddhist Association of Koshu City. Slowly the reconstruction of the Kin Zan temple began."

Roshi Keido Fukushima's eyes glow with excitement as he narrates the story of the rebuilding of the Kin Zan temple complex. There is no doubt that this project is one of the great achievements of his life. The first thing to be constructed was a road in order that the people could come up the mountain by automobiles. Slowly the construction of the main complex began. The Buddhists of Koshu City began collecting money and the resources to aid in the project. In 1999, Tofukuji in Kyoto celebrated 750th memorial services for the master Bukkan and invited a large delegation of the Chinese Buddhists to attend. In May 2000, through the efforts of the Roshi, 270 Japanese Buddhists visited the Kin Zan temple together. Presently the construction of the main complex, including eight big halls, has been completed. Roshi Fukushima is pleased that some lay people are beginning to come to the temple for ceremonies. Although currently there is no resident priest there, there are ten monks who live there. The images of Sakyamuni, Bodhisattvas, and other deities are in the process of being enshrined. To the Roshi's amazement, small villages and some shops are beginning to be visible in the vicinity. He sees that "as a good sign for the future of Kin Zan's development."

It was a momentous occasion for the Roshi when, on May 9, 1986, Prince Charles visited Tofukuji. He found the Prince to be "utterly charming and most delightful." Prince Charles was inquisitive and wanted to learn about the monastic life and sitting meditation. Roshi Fukushima seized the opportunity to give him a tour of the temple complex and also to tell him something about Zen. When the discussion centered on the monks, Prince Charles reportedly commented, "So they are training to have an empty mind, aren't they?" The Roshi remembers, "I thought, this is the chance. I passionately explained to him that the heart of Zen is *mushin*. It is usually translated as 'empty mind' or 'no mind' but that is not enough. I told him that when our mind is empty, we can accept and react to anything freely. So it is more appropriate to say that *mushin* is free mind, fresh mind, and creative mind." As they walked toward the main Zen garden, the Prince saw about twenty Zen monks and students meditating. He exclaimed, "Oh, wonderful!" He asked the Roshi many questions about Zen, which the Roshi answered. As they reached a porch, the media asked them to pose for a picture. The Prince was concerned whether this was a place of meditation. With his sense of humor, Keido responded, "No Sir, this is where you get your pictures taken." Both had a hearty laugh. Prince Charles overstayed his designated length of visit by fifteen minutes and enjoyed his tour. As they pleasantly parted company, Roshi Fukushima remarked, "Please come again and let us do *zazen* together," to which the Prince responded, "That is a good idea."

In 1989, Roshi Keido Fukushima turned his attention to the West. He was invited to give a series of lectures and calligraphy demonstrations at Kansas State University. He accepted the invitation and since then has been visiting the United States every year. Of course he had a standing invitation from the Claremont colleges ever since 1974. He decided to formally renew that relationship and included Claremont in his yearly visits. He recalls: "When I left Claremont in 1974, I had made myself a promise to return as a Zen master and do something for the American people. I am trying to fulfill that promise now."

Since 1974, several American students have visited Tofukuji to practice meditation. As his visits to the States increased, the number of American visitors to Tofukuji has also increased. The Roshi sought to informally formalize the relationship between Tofukuji and the American visitors by establishing what he calls "the Kyoto connection." Since he had spent time at Claremont colleges and enjoyed his interaction with students, he extended the invitation to American students to visit his monastery. The first such connection to be formed was the K-C connection (K for Kyoto and C for Claremont). To date, this relationship has been established with twenty-some colleges and universities that he visits every year. Several students and faculty have spent short as well as long terms at Tofukuji under this program. It is a unique initiative, but then Roshi Keido Fukushima is not an ordinary Zen master.

The Message
of the
Zen Master

The Ho-jo Garden at Tofukuji

Within the Zen tradition, a Zen master is a Buddha. His enlightenment is to be reflected through his life and message. In previous sections I have attempted to give a brief sketch of Roshi Keido Fukushima's life. In the following pages an attempt is made to summarize his message. For those well versed in Japanese, a detailed account of Keido's teachings can be ascertained through his writings.[1] Here I have relied on many of his lectures, conversations, discussions, and formal interviews. To achieve this goal I have taken certain phrases from his talks and lectures that he is very fond of, and used them as titles to summarize his insights about Zen Buddhism. Some of these phrases have also been the focus of his calligraphy as traditionally presented in *boku-seki* format. An example of his calligraphy is included to illustrate the Zen message as conveyed by these phrases. In ancient China and Japan, many Zen masters became famous for their art as a medium of Zen expression. This tradition still continues. Roshi Keido Fukushima is exemplary in this tradition.

As far as his message is concerned, Keido's teachings are derived from Zen Buddhism in general, and Rinzai in particular. As such, there is nothing new to present. However, his uniqueness lies in the manner in which he presents his ideas. For me, the most significant aspect of this presentation is how he applies the Zen ideals in his own life, and how I have observed him. I have studied Buddhism and taught Zen in various classes for a long time. What my students have found mean-

---

[1] Keido Fukushima has authored several books in Japanese. The English titles are: *Zen is a Religion of Mu, Free Mind, Satori in Mushin, Mind of Hok-ku-kyo* (sutra). He is in the process of completing *My Life as a Zen Master*. All these works are in Japanese.

ingful is the reflection of Zen ideals in the lives of those who live it. For me, the examples have come from Tofukuji and its head abbot, Keido Fukushima.

I once asked him, "How is Zen lived in your daily life?" He replied, "Every moment of my life is lived by Zen principles. I am not separated from Zen. So from the moment I wake up till the moment I go to sleep, I am living by Zen. I am not conscious that I am *applying* Zen. Since my awakening [his experience at Nanzenji], I am Zen." I probed further, "Do you behave in a certain way with your training monks which is different from the way you behave with your friends and guests?" He responded, "Of course there is a difference in mannerism since we have to follow the monastery rules at Tofukuji. We all have to follow a certain discipline, which the lay people do not. But, for me, the monks, friends, and guests are all equal. They all have Buddha nature, and I treat them as such." "So, what does that mean?" I asked. "It means that I am compassionate toward all beings," he responded. I agreed that indeed he was.

In subsequent pages the reader is introduced to Roshi Fukushima's message through his calligraphy and teachings. He has numerous phrases from the Zen tradition that he has made the subject of his calligraphy and Zen teachings. Here I have selected five such phrases that he is so fond of using. These are:

- Every Day is a Fine Day
- Hey! Throw It Away
- Be a Fool
- With My Zen Mind
- Watch, Touch, and Bite

For me these simple phrases beautifully summarize Fukushima's Zen and introduce us to his mind.

"Every Day is a Fine Day"
Calligraphy by Roshi Keido Fukushima

Every Day is a Fine Day

It was a nasty day. It had been raining all day. I had been waiting to play golf all week, and now all plans for golf had to be cancelled. I was in a bad mood. All I could think of was, "Why did it have to rain today?" Suddenly Gensho walked into the living room, all drenched with rain, and with a big smile shouted, "Every day is a fine day." I remember that I said nothing to his exuberant comment. On the contrary—I was irritated, thinking, "How can it be a fine day when it's raining cats and dogs and I can't play golf." This incident occurred in 1974 at Claremont. Ever since that day, on numerous occasions, I have heard Roshi Keido Fukushima use this phrase—"Every Day is a Fine Day"—in his talks on Zen. Now that I understand the Zen import of this phrase, I have often greeted my students in my classes on a cold, wintry day in Ohio with the remark, "Every day is a fine day." It presents an opportunity for a good discussion. As for me, I can cancel a tee-time for a golf game without getting a headache.

So, what does Zen have to do with the weather? The Roshi explains that it was Ummon (864 - 949 C.E.), a T'ang dynasty Zen master in China, who was fond of using this phrase. Keido has made it his phrase because it gives an insight into Zen life. The average person is not free to embrace life "as it is." We always look at life dualistically, in terms of "good" and "bad." A rainy day may be bad for a golfer, but a beautiful day for a farmer. On the other hand, too much sun might be bad for both of them. The inability to transcend this dualism produces suffering. It could be physical or psychological. When I could not play golf due to rain on that day in California, it made me angry, frustrated, anxious, unfriendly, moody, and withdrawn. Besides, it gave me a headache. This is a relatively minor problem compared to some serious events that life presents to us. What if we lose a loved one? How does it affect us?

Zen teaches us to be free from dualities in order to be what we are meant to be. The real question is—why do we view life dualistically, in terms of "good" and "bad"? Roshi Fukushima explains that it is due to "ego." Ego veils reality from its true essence (which Buddhism explains in terms of non-essence). Rather, it distorts reality in an attempt to perceive what it wants to perceive, not *what is*. In the Taoist tradition, it is likened to the carving of the "uncarved block"—the symbol for the Tao. Lao Tzu (6th century B.C.E.) warned his disciples not to carve the block lest they change the Tao. This is also discussed by Shankara (788 - 820 C.E.), one of the great philosophers of India. He discussed this in the context of *maya* (temporary reality) and its relation to Brahman (ultimate Reality). He warned against the problem of "superimposition" (*vivartavada*). He was concerned that living in *maya* (phenomenal reality), *jiva* (ego-self) superimposes its own interpretation of reality onto reality. Thus, Brahman remains hidden, and *maya* is viewed as ultimate. Buddha viewed this as the problem of "ignorant craving," which is the cause of suffering. One can argue that "ego" is necessary for self-preservation. Freud viewed the function of the ego as a mediator between the super-ego and the id. It provided a balance between the two extremes. In Zen, as in Buddhism as a whole, ego is perceived to be an artificial condition. It does not have a true identity. It is the creation of the mind.

For Roshi Fukushima, in order to enjoy a "free" life, one must become a person of "no-ego." He explains: "This is what in Japan we call *mu-no-hito* [a person of *mu*]. *Mu* refers to 'no-ego.' When you become a person of *mu*, you can *adjust* to bad and good things freely. You can *adapt* to all conditions without worrying about the consequences freely. It also means that you can *accept* the good and the bad freely." An average person (person of ego) wants to accept only the good of his own interpretation and avoid the bad of his own interpretation. In the process, s/he misses both.

I once asked the Roshi, "Should we not avoid the bad and do what is good?" His answer reflected the notion that Zen is not antinomian.[2] "Of course Zen believes in the *dharma* [ethics]," he said, "but for Zen it is the question of how one arrives at *dharma*." An ordinary person accepts the good (*dharma*) without transcending the dualism of good and bad. This is the sign of ego. Of course, Zen condemns what is bad, and embraces what is good, but only after having transcended both. The ability to distinguish the "good" as good and the "bad" as bad comes after the Zen awakening. Thus, merely believing or understanding the necessity to "transcend" is not enough. Zen calls for an "experience."

When I spent an extended period of time in the *sodo* (monk's quarters) at Tofukuji, I discovered that becoming *mu* (*mu-no-hito*) was the main preoccupation of the training monks. During the first year of their three years of minimum training to become a priest, they were constantly hammered with the notion of becoming *mu* (an ego-less person). The Roshi explained that when the monks first enter the monastery, they have often never heard of the term *mu*. When they begin the *koan* study, the first *koan* they are likely to be given is "Joshu's *mu*." For weeks they can be observed asking each other, "*Mu*? What in the world is *mu*?" Once they understand it, they are encouraged to experience it. This is known as "becoming *mu*." Once they become *mu*, life changes; they develop a higher perspective and understand the dualistic nature of life. The Roshi was emphatic in saying, "In the monastery we work very hard together to generate the experience of *mu* in our monks. This is the first step in understanding Zen." Indeed, I was able to see how the monks in the monastery lived the lives of ego-less selves.

---

[2] Antinomianism (*anti*, against; *nomos*, law): the term is used to designate freedom from religious law or external regulations to human living. In a negative sense it implies that if one experiences *satori* (enlightenment), one is no longer subjected to *dharma* (religious law). Keido does not hold this view.

It reflected in their acts of compassion towards each other and towards me. "That is the key," I thought, "When ego leaves, the vacuum is filled with compassion." Later I learned that although it is a mental experience, it has a physical dimension as well. One monk describes this experience as "feeling the compassion in the *hara* [solar plexis]." When I was leaving Tofukuji in November 2001, the Roshi offered me a box containing a gift. Inside the box was a ceramic teacup with the Roshi's own calligraphy. It read, "*Mu* [in Japanese character] for Dr. Ishwar." I was deeply moved. The Roshi had a good laugh.

The Roshi remarks that the teaching of *mu* (no-ego) is not peculiar to Zen. First, it comes out of the teachings of Sakyamuni Buddha (563 - 483 B.C.E.). Second, it is also found in the world's other great religions. In the teachings of the Buddha, the Four Noble Truths, which identify the cause and cure of suffering, the problem of ego is at the heart of Buddha's discussion. The second Noble Truth, which identifies "ignorant craving" as the cause of suffering, automatically implies that cravings are linked with ego. Consequently the control of cravings is impossible without the control of ego. Within the Theravada tradition, which was formulated after the death of the Buddha, when the elders of the tradition set forth certain doctrines of Buddhism, they included *anatta* (no-self) as a part of the doctrine of Three Signs.[3] *Anatta* was further explained by the doctrine of *skandhas*, which suggests that what is perceived as "self" is the ever-changing interaction of five aggregates. The *skandhas* do not have an independent reality of their own since they are constantly changing. One of the imports of this doctrine is that if there is no permanent self, there is no permanent ego. Some Buddhist writers have gone so far as to say that ego is a pure illusion; it does not exist. *Nirvana* (no more burning), then, in the Theravada tradition, is a state of extinction of all

---

[3] In Theravada Buddhism, the Three Signs are: *anatta* (no-self), *anicca* (impermanence), and *dukkha* (suffering).

desires. However, this extinction is not reserved for an after-death experience only. *Nirvana* can be experienced while a person is still living. If the Buddha could do it, so can the lay people.

The problem of ego is also recognized in other religions like Christianity, Hinduism, and Islam. Jesus' admonitions "to deny yourself to find yourself," and "to become like a child to inherit the kingdom of God," point in this direction. Furthermore, his own confrontation with Satan in the wilderness in which he defeated Satan can be compared with Siddhartha's battle with Mara.[4] In both cases they were victorious over their own egotistical affirmations. In Hinduism, from the *Upanishads* to the *Bhagavadgita*, there is a clear indication that ego hides the true nature of God. The yoga tradition is a clear example of how without self-control the experience of *samadhi* is an impossibility. Within Islam, the Sufi tradition clearly states that *fana* is the highest experience where all individuality (including ego) is lost in God. Needless to say, the mystical traditions within all world religions have addressed the problem of ego, and have found it to be an impediment to spiritual experience. However, within the Zen tradition, the extinguishing of ego or the experience of *satori* is not perceived as mystical. Roshi Fukushima suggests, "There is nothing mystical about Zen. Those people who are outside the tradition, and who have not had an awakening, envision the experience as mystical. For Zen, the experiences are merely *natural.* There is nothing mystical about them."

During my discussions with the Roshi, I wanted to know how one controls or extinguishes the ego. I was concerned that the metaphysical solution of the problem that "ego is merely 'illusory' and therefore do not attach to it," may not satisfy an average individual. For us the problem is real. The Roshi agreed and

---

[4] For a description of Jesus' temptations, see the gospel according to Matthew 4:1-10.

pointed out that in Zen there are practical suggestions to handle the problem. Of course knowing the tradition and the development of Buddhism may help to understand the problem, but to experience "ego-lessness," one must do something. "The primary exercise in Zen to get rid of ego is *zazen*," he said. "Where do the desires and ego originate?" he asked. "They originate in our minds." *Zazen* is a way to empty the mind. It is no more than that. It is a way to penetrate into the unconscious, "where the seeds of all evil lie," he continued.

The chanting of the *mantra* is another way. Traditional Buddhism puts a great deal of emphasis on chanting the *sutras*. Some of the benefits are described in meritorious ways—to appease the souls of the dead, to gain good karma, etc. But chanting has another function that is very practical. "In chanting one loses oneself in the act itself. There is a loss of consciousness of 'I,' 'me,' and 'mine,'" explains the Roshi. At Tofukuji, *sutra* chanting begins very early in the morning, soon after the wake-up bell at 3:00 a.m. I recall how hesitant I was to participate in this ritual, not because it was so early in the morning, but because I did not understand the language. However after several days of participation, which included merely listening to the monks on my part, I began to enjoy my participation. The rhythm of the wooden drum, the sound of the gong, and the sound of chanting began to penetrate my whole being. Often I lost track of the time. Something in me was lost momentarily.

Although *zazen* and chanting are primary means of experiencing the loss of self, *koan* meditation is equally important. In the Rinzai sect of Zen, much significance is attached to *koan* meditation. The Roshi explains: "When an answer to the *koan* comes, it is not through the rational mind which operates dualistically. It comes when the individual can tap into another level of reality and shut off one's own ego self."

I asked the Roshi if the collecting of the alms that monks did on a regular basis could function as a deterrent to nurturing ego. He responded by saying, "Many people call this ritual 'begging.' It is not. It is not easy to go out and ask people to give you something. It is a form of meditation. Yes, a young person with a strong ego cannot do it. It is an exercise in reducing ego." I understood what the Zen master meant. I had followed the Tofukuji monks in the streets surrounding the monastery and taken some pictures. I wanted to participate in their rounds around town, but could not bring myself to do it. Soon I learned that only monks could go on the collection rounds.

Furthermore, one of the basic requirements to become a monk was to shave the head. Traditionally in eastern cultures, hair has been viewed as a symbol of vanity. In Theravada Buddhism (which is very much like Zen), when a person's head is shaved, he is made to hold a few pieces of hair in his hand as a reminder of the control of pride and vanity. Receiving a monk's robe, giving up one's family, giving up one's given name, getting rid of possessions, sleeping on the floor, eating simple food, keeping up with the monastic vows—all such things are designed for the purpose of creating a new being, a being that will master his ego.

Generally we think of the problem of ego confined to an individual. In a lecture given at the College of Wooster in 2001, Roshi Fukushima, while discussing the problems created by the ego, addressed the issue of "national ego." He emphasized that nations often develop a unique sense of pride and become oppressive towards others. That kind of chauvinism can be a hindrance to world peace. He asked his audience to struggle against this national pride. He pointed out that in the past Japan was victimized by national pride and paid a heavy price for it. He warned that many industrial nations today are faced with this problem. Whether it is in the realm of economics, military, or culture, when a powerful nation misuses its power and forces others to capitulate, it is a consequence of a national ego. During the question and answer period, one student posed the question, "How can we confront our national ego which suppresses women, ethnic minorities, and the poor?" The Roshi responded by saying, "Of course, first you have to examine your own ego, then find the likeminded people to work with you. This is hard work, but it must be done. I wish you luck."

When the terrorists attacked the Twin Towers in New York City on September 11, 2001, I was staying at Tofukuji. During my regular interview with the Roshi, I asked him how he felt about the terrorists. "Bad ego," he exclaimed. "I can say to the terrorists that you are 'bad.' You have bad 'ego' because your actions are full of hate and violence, and you are killing innocent people." I continued, "How should we deal with the terrorists?" He remarked, "The Zen way would be to show our compassion. Zen believes that the Buddha nature is in everyone, including the bad person." I mentioned that Mahatma Gandhi believed that even Hitler could have a change of heart, and that Gandhi sent a letter to Hitler to stop killing the Jews. "Zen would be close to the Gandhian approach," the Roshi remarked.

During the same conversation I asked him how lay people could control their egos. I mentioned to him that the monks had the luxury of time. They could do all forms of meditation and experience the state of ego-lessness. Lay people have so many responsibilities and very little time. The Zen master paused and said, "It is a matter of degree. Of course, the lay people cannot practice like the monks, but they can begin by reading books, listening to Zen lectures, and practicing meditation. A little bit of effort will produce results." He further explained, "If everyone took time to examine their egos and control their cravings, this world would be a better place." He began to narrate many instances in his life when he had changed the lives of people by teaching them the Zen way. While others had condemned these people, the Roshi accepted them and taught them to be compassionate. According to him, "Their lives changed and they became better people." "Does Zen believe in counseling?" I asked. He responded by saying, "Well, there is no special Zen counseling. I only teach what Buddhism teaches. Within those teachings there are solutions to many problems."

So, what does Zen have to do with the weather? When I posed this question to the Roshi, he laughed and said, "Well, Zen will say: When it rains, take an umbrella. When there is too much sun, wear a hat. When it snows, put on your boots. Don't complain, because every day is a fine day." Failure to do so is to invite suffering.

"Hey! Throw It Away"
Calligraphy by Roshi Keido Fukushima

Hey! Throw It Away

In my office, behind the door, there is a long scroll with Keido Fukushima's calligraphy. It reads (in Chinese characters), "Hey! Throw it away." It is there as a constant reminder of my "attachments."

When I asked Keido why he had chosen this theme as a topic of his calligraphy, he said that in this particular teaching, he was inspired by the famous Zen master, Joshu (Chao-chou 778-897 C.E.). I knew that the Roshi had studied Joshu at Otani University and in his talks he was fond of quoting from Joshu. When I probed further, he narrated a famous incident that involved Joshu and one of his disciples. Evidently, in a conversation with Joshu, the disciple said that he had taken off all of his illusions, and now what should he do? Joshu responded, "Throw it away." At once the student retorted, "I already told you that I have no illusions." At this Joshu, in his Zen mind, responded, "Okay, keep it." Upon hearing Joshu's response, the disciple was enlightened. In this story, Joshu, as a Zen master, realized that his disciple was attached to unconscious illusions of which he was not aware. So, Joshu asked him to throw them away. When the disciple persisted that he had no illusions, Joshu asked him to carry on. Luckily, Joshu's disciple had the insight to recognize that his master was not attached to his own answer, as he asked the disciple to "carry on." Realizing this Zen mind, the disciple was enlightened.

Roshi Fukushima explains that Zen focuses on two types of attachments—conscious and unconscious. It is easy to recognize conscious attachments but very difficult to be cognizant of the unconscious ones. Consequently, people may think that they should be happy because they are detached from many material things, but still remain unhappy. It is because they are unconsciously attached to many things, including the desire for detachment. Even the monks are faced with this danger. That is why the winter *sesshin* (usually in December) is very critical in Zen training. The Roshi remarks: "During the winter *sesshin*, which is so tough and abnormal, I can tell whether or not the monks have penetrated their unconscious minds. Usually during the *koan* study in *sesshin*, I can tell whether a monk has experienced his first *satori*. Those who do break through have a unique experience and can truly 'throw it away.'" When I mentioned to him that there seemed to be a similarity between Zen and psychoanalysis, the Roshi agreed but pointed out one major difference. "Through psychoanalysis what is restored as a healthy self is an ego-laden self. This is not the case in Zen. Detachment comes through the experience of ego-lessness. However, a 'restored self' can work to obtain egoless self," he added.

Keido points out that getting rid of unconscious illusions is most difficult. He states: "Only after taking off the unconscious illusion does one have the realization that s/he had unconscious illusions. Therefore the Zen training must continue even after the first *satori* experience."

In the Rinzai sect generally, it takes ten years to complete *koan* study. After completion of the study, the disciple must continue for ten years of private study. In the monastery, the master can catch the problem of unconscious illusions. However, during private studies, there is always the danger of new illusions setting in. When I asked the Roshi if the problem of attachments can happen to a Zen master, he responded, "Yes, there is a possibility of many attachments dealing with money, sex, power, etc. Therefore a good Zen master continues in his practice. There are also cases when a Zen master refuses to select an heir because he realizes the problem of attachment in a disciple. As I said before, Zen demands a strict training."

The problem of attachment is linked with the problem of ego. It is for this reason that Buddhism emphasizes the doctrine of *anatta* (no-self). In Buddhist psychology, there is a clear understanding how desire arises due to ego. When desire arises, the human tendency is to quench it by fulfilling it. The next time the desire returns with a higher magnitude. Fulfilling the new desire now requires more energy and resources. Having fulfilled this, the intensity of the desire increases and the process continues. The end result of this cycle is that ultimately the individual finds himself suffocating in the web of desires. The fulfillment of desires produces attachments. Some of these attachments (illusions) remain on the conscious level; others find their place in the unconscious mind. The end result is suffering. The pervasive materialism so prevalent in modern economies is based on the assumption that the more we consume, the happier we will be. The advertisers on radio, TV, and the internet send us the same message—buy more and you will be happy. The needs are created artificially and we are told that it is good for our economy. Buddhist economics challenges this norm. It asserts that the sellers, through their advertisements, attack where human nature is weak. They manipulate and capitalize on the weakness of the need to quench desires.

When I posed this problem to Roshi Fukushima, he understood the dilemma but asserted that the problem was an ancient one. After all, this is what Siddhartha Gautama discovered under the Bodhi tree. It seems that he was able to transcend the consequences that stem from attachments. For the average individual the web of desires produces physical and mental suffering even though s/he may not realize it. Buddhism, including Zen, teaches the method of nullifying the effects of attachments. To handle the problem, both *dhyana* (meditation) and *prajna* (wisdom) are necessary. The wisdom comes from understanding the Buddha *dharma*. Meditation provides an exercise in self-purification. The Roshi recognizes that although minimization of wants is a Buddhist ideal, certain desires and wants are necessary for survival. Therefore, the vows that a lay person takes are less severe than the ones taken by the monks and nuns. However, the goal for both is ultimately the same—to transcend all attachments.

The Roshi explains that a distinction can be made between "good" attachments and "bad" attachments. For example, to covet a neighbor's wealth is a bad attachment, but to seek *nirvana* is a good attachment. However on a higher level of spiritual development, even desiring *nirvana* is perceived as a bad attachment. He points out that when the monks first come to Tofukuji, they may be motivated to have a Zen experience (*satori*). In fact they should think positively about having an enlightenment experience. But in the later stages of training, all talk about *satori* is given up. I found this to be true. Once when I asked a senior monk if he was close to *satori* experience, the response was, "ha-ha-ha."

The Zen tradition is replete with many anecdotes and stories that bring the problem of attachment closer to home. For example, consider the following question, "If you are walking down the street and meet the Buddha, what do you do?" "Kill him," comes the answer. How absurd! Can we really kill the Buddha? Obviously the import of this saying is that one has to kill the attachment to the Buddha. Another story has two monks warming themselves on a cold wintry night by chopping and burning statues of the Buddha. Again, what they are burning is their attachment to the images. One of my favorites is the story of two monks who come upon a stream that they have to cross. Standing by the stream is a young maiden who also wants to go across. Seeing her dilemma, one monk picks her up and wades across, puts her on the other shore, and continues walking. The other monk, witnessing the event, finally breaks the silence by protesting that the other monk had touched the woman. He had surely broken the monastic rule that prohibits association with women. The monk's reply to his friend's protest is most telling. He says, "Oh! I left the girl near the shore. It seems you are still carrying her." Once again the message is clear. One should not be attached to rules as well. Does that mean that the rules should not be observed or deliberately broken? Not at all. The point is: at what stage of spiritual progress can one see the Buddha and *dharma* as mediums— vehicles (*yanas*) to reach the shore of *nirvana*.

In the preface to the book *Zen Mind, Beginners Mind,* Huston Smith narrates an incident when he visited Roshi Shunryu Suzuki.[5] While they were talking, Huston Smith remarked that in his teachings, the Roshi didn't talk much about *satori*. Upon hearing this, Mrs. Suzuki remarked, "Because he has not had one." Shunryu Suzuki laughed and said, "Do not tell any one." This is yet another example of living in the spirit of detachment.

In Buddaghosa's text, *Visuddhimagga* ("The Path of Purity"), there is discussion on the "recollection of death." The text describes the various ways in which death approaches and terrifies human beings. The monks and nuns are expected to contemplate on the text as an exercise in meditation. It is interesting to note how Buddhaghosa describes the benefits of this exercise. He states:

> And the monk who is devoted to this recollection of death is always watchful, he feels disgust for all forms of becoming, he forsakes the hankering after life, he disapproves of evil, he does not hoard up many things, and with regard to the necessities of life he is free from the taint of stinginess. He gains familiarity with the notion of impermanence, and, when he follows that up, also the notions of ill and not-self will stand out to him.[6]

---

[5] Shunryu Suzuki (d. 1971 C.E.) was one of the leading Zen masters of Soto Zen, who founded the Zen Center of San Francisco, CA, USA.

[6] The quote is taken from "Buddhaghosa on the Recollection of Death," (translated by Edward Conze) as it appears in Roger Eastman, *The Ways of Religion* (New York: Oxford University Press, 3rd edition, 1999), p. 110.

It is clear that this section of the text emphasizes the importance of non-attachment for a religious life. It also reflects on the problem of ego (no-self).

As I discussed the issue of attachment with the Roshi, he enunciated the Buddhist teachings on permanence and impermanence. The issue is: how does attachment (to ideas, doctrines, things, etc.) become the cause of suffering? Buddhism affirms that there is nothing in life that is permanent. All of reality is in constant change; so there is nothing that one can attach to. We often hear that the Greek philosopher, Heraclitus (c.540 - c.470 B.C.E.), who believed in the impermanent nature of things, supposedly said, "You can never step in the same stream twice," meaning that the second time one steps into the stream, the water has already flowed—the reality has changed. The Buddhist response to this saying would be, "You cannot step in the same stream even *once*, let alone twice." This is to emphasize that nothing is the same; that change is occurring all the time. The doctrine of impermanence (*anicca*) is further explained by the notion of dependent co-origination (*praticcasamuppada*). It suggests that impermanence is due to the link of the chain of cause and effect. Those who do not see the impermanent nature of things attach to them thinking that they are permanent. This is caused by their ignorance (*avidya*).

The problem of attachment is ultimately connected with the notion of *shunyata* (emptiness) as discussed by Nagarjuna (2nd century C.E.). He asserted that if Theravada Buddhism believed in the doctrine of *anatta* (*anatman* = no-self in the Hindu sense), it automatically negated the existence of Brahman (the supreme soul = God). Furthermore, the concept of *anicca* (impermanence) denied the permanence of any reality. For Nagarjuna, the logical consequence of this line of thinking was that all was *shunya* (empty). Despite the fact that the *yogacara* school dismissed the notion of *shunyata* as a concept existing in the mind, and proposed the notion of *alaya vijnana* (store house of consciousness) as the source of all concepts, Nagarjuna's notion of *shunyata* gained philosophical credence and became the backbone of Ch'an in China and Zen in Japan. Thus, for Zen, the awakening (*kensho* in Japanese) or *satori* is an experience of *shunyata*, not a merger of the individual soul with a higher soul. In this manner, the notion of detachment is given a philosophical base and it becomes the foundation of Zen spiritual life. When I asked the Roshi if the monks understood Nagarjuna's philosophy, he remarked, "Most of the monks do their undergraduate study in Buddhism and therefore are familiar with Buddhist philosophical development. However, in the monastery we do not discuss philosophy. We work hard to give them an experience." I understood his point and proposed that perhaps the motto of Tofukuji ought to be "experience first, philosophy later."

Working with the Buddhist ideal of non-attachment in the classroom, I often find that students misunderstand this concept. They understand what attachment means, but detachment poses a problem. For most, detachment suggests such meanings as escaping, running away, foregoing, being in isolation, etc. To them it means being irresponsible and emotionally non-engaged in daily life. The Roshi refutes such an understanding. Detachment or non-attachment does not mean being irresponsible or disinterested in daily life. In the spirit of the *Bhagavadgita*, it means non-attachment to the fruits of one's action. It means keeping the ego out when undertaking a task. Actions undertaken with selfish motives divert the focus from the action itself to the individual. Once the actor (individual) becomes the focus, the spirit of altruism is lost. In the process the individual hurts himself and the neighbor.

Often students will ask, "Do Buddhists ever have fun?" To them it seems that the qualities of non-ego, non-attachment, and self-control will lead to a very dull life. If this were the case, Buddhists would be the saddest people on the face of the earth.

On the contrary, they express contentment and joy. For the Zen master, the Buddhist understanding of happiness is not based on gratification, in the sense that happiness comes when all desires are fulfilled. Happiness takes on a new meaning when desires are controlled and the egotistical self is given up.

Does non-attachment mean that one should not possess the good things that life has to offer? Can a lay person, who has all the luxuries of life, still practice Buddhist non-attachment? According to the Roshi, one can. When I probed further, he responded by stating, "This is the problem of the degree to which one is dependent on the 'stuff' one possesses. Can the person exercise letting go in the midst of having it all? If the person can, then he is not controlled by the 'stuff' he has. Then letting go will cause no pain. He is not attached."

In Buddhism it is important to make a distinction between desire and craving. To my mind, craving is that stage of human experience when the desire becomes an addiction. An addiction implies that the one addicted has lost self-control. The thing that one is addicted to now controls the individual. Such is the case with an alcoholic or a drug addict. The loss of self-control leads to the loss of the power of discrimination. Thus the mind is defiled. In Zen, a particular attention needs to be given to the state of mind.

Keido Fukushima's calligraphy, "Hey! Throw it away," which hangs in my office, is a constant reminder to me about my attachments and my ability and inability to throw them away. I could not resist asking the Roshi if he had any attachments of his own. He laughed and said, "I have many good attachments. I like coffee, chocolate, and Joan Baez." He then narrated an incident. In the sixties, he listened to Joan Baez and liked her songs. Some of his friends periodically gave him Baez's records, and he has a good collection of them. Recently, when he was in New York, through the internet his interpreter discovered that Baez was giving a concert in New York. The Roshi, along with his assistant and the interpreter, went to the concert. "I really enjoyed her singing. She is my new attachment," he said laughingly. Knowing the Roshi as I do, I know that he is not addicted to coffee, chocolate, or Joan Baez. He can throw them away anytime.

"Be a Fool"
Calligraphy by Roshi Keido Fukushima

Be a Fool

In the annals of Chinese Zen (Ch'an), there is a tradition about an Indian monk, Bodhidharma, who brought Ch'an to China. He is said to have meditated in a cave for nine years to such an extent that his legs became paralyzed. Today in Japan one can buy *dharma* dolls that have no legs, and are a favorite of children. Bodhidharma is recognized as the first patriarch of Zen and his teachings have been responsible for establishing the following axioms for Zen spirituality:

1. A special transmission outside the scripture.
2. No dependence upon words and letters.
3. Direct pointing to the soul of man.
4. Seeing into one's nature and attainment of Buddhahood.[7]

The first two statements recorded in these axioms speak to the limitation of the rational mind. The second, in particular, points to the limitations of philosophy, which celebrate reason and logic. In order to illustrate this point, my own professor, the late John A. Hutchison at Claremont Graduate School, was fond of saying, "Zen is a philosophy of having no philosophy." I remember writing an essay on this statement during one of the examinations. The Zen *koans*, stories, and art are full of examples which emphasize the limitations of the rational mind.

Roshi Keido Fukushima tells his own story as to how he was made aware of the limitations of his rational mind when he entered Nanzenji as a monk. First, he was told to leave his accumulated knowledge behind when he joined the monastery. He

---

[7] John A. Hutchison, *Paths of Faith* (New York: McGraw-Hill Book Co., 1969), p. 244.

recalls, "I cried all night. At that time I was a Ph.D. student at Otani University, and the thought of forgetting everything I had learned was quite disturbing. I decided to enter the monastery anyway." However, the real awakening to the fact that he had to transcend his rational mind came to him during his *koan* study. As is the tradition in Rinzai Zen, Keido began his *koan* study with his master, Roshi Shibayama. He gave what he thought were the best answers to his *koan*, only to be rejected by his master. Often Roshi Shibayama would ring his bell to end the *dokusan* (*koan* interview) before Keido could finish his answer. Each time he would bring his best thought-out answer based on his studies of the *Lin-chi Records*. Shibayama would remark, "You know the *Lin-chi Records* really well" and then reject the answer. Sometimes he would end the *dokusan* by sarcastically saying, "Oh! You are studying well." Finally Keido thought that the *Lin-chi Records* which he had studied thoroughly had no good answers for *koan*s so he must seek knowledge elsewhere. However, he did not pass his *koan*. This went on for two years. During the third year of the *koan* study, Roshi Shibayama asked Keido during the *dokusan* to become a fool. Recalling that evening, he states, "Be a fool, Shibayama Roshi said. I did not know what that meant. So I asked my fellow monks [who had passed their *koan*] if they were instructed to be a fool. 'No,' they said. But, they were told to 'study hard.'" Keido laughs.

Keido came to a rude awakening that he was attached to his knowledge. What that really meant was that he had not learned to exhaust his rational mind. When Roshi Shibayama taunted him saying, "Perhaps you should return to Otani University to continue studying," he then realized that the problem was not with the *Lin-chi Records*, but with himself. He came to the realization that he had an unconscious attachment to knowledge. Gradually he realized his problem and decided to become a fool. "In December of my third year of *koan* study," he remembers, "finally one evening Shibayama responded to my answer to the *koan* by stating, 'it is good.'" From then on the *koan* studies went smoothly and Keido made consistent progress, surpassing his fellow monks.

When I listen to Roshi Keido Fukushima's lectures, the theme of "becoming a fool" is often repeated. This is particularly true when he is addressing American students. He is keen on insisting that students are in the business of accumulating rational knowledge and so are their professors. He admits that rational knowledge is functional, but functional only in a limited sense. Like Aldous Huxley, he insists that rationality can bring one to the door of a room, but something else is needed to help one enter it.[8] That something other is *intuition*. Roshi Fukushima explains that by intuition he does not mean premonition, or the feeling that something is going to happen. That is a general understanding of the term intuition. In Zen, intuition is believed to be a faculty of the mind. This faculty opens up when the rational mind is spent. The imagery of the rational mind would be like a compressed coil of spring, full of tension, but which is pressed against a block waiting to be released. The release will come only when the block is removed and the spring jumps forward, unleashing all its power until it comes to a state of rest. In this example, the compressed spring denotes the condition of the rational mind, the block represents its limitations, and release, the freedom which is experienced through intuitive mind.

As stated earlier, in Zen Buddhism, rationality is associated with ego. Unless the ego is conquered, attachment to knowledge will remain. For professors and students, this is the most difficult lesson to learn. However, ultimately, every student has to ask the fundamental question, "Is my knowledge all there is?" For some, it is quite evident that it is "wisdom," not "knowledge" that will see them through life's journey. Without wisdom, there is a danger of the misuse of knowledge. Often when I ask my students to differentiate between knowledge and wisdom, the most common response is that knowledge is acquired, but wisdom comes from experience. The Zen response is somewhat like this.

---

[8] Aldous Huxley's thesis can be found in his book, *The Doors of Perception.*

It calls for an experience. After the experience, the acquired knowledge is not forgotten, but retained with a higher perspective. The reader will recall that when Keido was asked to forsake his knowledge to become a Zen monk, he cried all night. He later came to the realization that his knowledge was not wasted or forgotten. He puts it in this manner, "First I thought that giving up knowledge meant becoming stupid. However, after the Zen experience, I realized that my knowledge did not disappear. I now understand more clearly."

In the context of Zen there is a true story that has been mentioned in many books. The event took place in Japan. A scholar had gone to Japan to study Zen. When he was granted an interview with a Zen master, the Roshi served him some tea. As he filled the scholar's cup, he did not stop there, but kept pouring until the tea spilled beyond the cup to the table, and to the floor. Finally the scholar could not contain himself and screamed, "Please stop." At this point, the Zen master stated that the condition of the scholar's mind was like the teacup. It was overflowing with ideas and concepts. He was instructed to empty his mind if he wanted to learn about Zen. Likewise the story of Eugen Herrigel is well known. Herrigel came to Japan to study Zen, but was subjected to practicing archery for six years. In his book, *Zen and the Art of Archery*, Herrigel narrates his odyssey with the bow and arrows. After three years of practice, he was instructed to begin again because he had not yet conquered his rational mind. At one point, his teacher refused to instruct him because Herrigel had mastered the technique of shooting and was hitting the target, but had not learned to "let go of his mind." Once he followed his teacher's instructions to let go, he experienced the Zen of archery. One day his teacher exclaimed, "It shot." Herrigel had the unique experience of his arrow leaving the bow as if of its own volition. As Roshi Fukushima would say, "He finally shot with his no-mind."

In 1998, when I first spent five weeks at Tofukuji, I met an American jazz musician who had come there to participate in a week of intensive meditation (*sesshin*). Evidently he had been coming to Tofukuji for a long time ever since he had been a student at Pomona College in Claremont. I once asked him how his practice of Zen (particularly *zazen*) had improved his playing of the saxophone. He could not identify any single thing but mentioned that he played effortlessly and his music flowed more spontaneously. This was particularly true after he went back to New York having spent some time at Tofukuji. He also remarked that his fellow musicians noticed the change in his playing and often acknowledged that this was due to his frequent trips to the Zen monastery in Japan. When I discussed this musician's experience with the Roshi, he said, "He plays with his no-mind."

In 2001, when I spent three months at Tofukuji, I had a minor experience that I would like to share. I do not claim to have had a *satori* experience or even anything coming close to that. However, during my *koan* study, I did have an experience which has special significance for me. The reader will recall that I had been given the *koan* called "Joshu's *mu*" to solve. My rational mind went through many convulsions as I tried to find an answer that would satisfy the Zen master. I often expressed my frustration to Jeff Shore of Hanazono University, whom I had befriended. He advised me to be patient and keep on working on the *koan*. After a long struggle, one evening I gave an answer during the *dokusan* which seemed to have come from somewhere other than my rational mind. While struggling with the rational mind brought frustration, the letting go brought peace and joy. On a later date when I mentioned this to the Zen master, he remarked, "Since you are a professor, it is good for you to experience the limitations of the rational mind."

Zen places no exclusive claim to the working of the intuitive mind in everyday experiences. These experiences can and do occur naturally, but we do not put much emphasis on them. Even Einstein is reported to have said that the solutions to many of the problems on which he worked came not when he was rationally working them out. Rather, the answer often came when he was doing something else or resting. The average person can testify to this truth. What Zen wants to do is to extend the intensity of these experiences in our lives. These are not *satori* experiences, but point to the possibility of the reality of *satori*. For *satori*, Zen training is an absolute necessity for the average person. Once when I was discussing this issue with Roshi Fukushima, he recalled that many American students have asked him if it is possible to gain a *satori* experience after a short stay at the monastery. He believes that minor, so-called "psychological" experiences may occur during *zazen* practice, but these are not *satori*. I myself had some such experiences. Once in my room at Tofukuji, I woke up with so much clarity of mind that I read a book on Zen for two hours without getting tired, and understood everything I had read. On another occasion, while eating a meal with the monks in the dining hall, I happened to look at my soup bowl. To my amazement I saw many colorful designs in the tiny bubbles in the soup. On another occasion, while waiting for *dokusan* outside the Roshi's room, I felt a profound sense of peace and joy. The feeling was so intense that at the moment I did not care if I had a job or a family. The Zen master put no special significance to these experiences. For me, nonetheless, they point to the limitations of the rational mind. Enjoyable as they are, they can prove to be a hindrance to Zen awakening if one attaches too much significance to them. This is the lesson I have learned from Roshi Fukushima.

Since Zen advocates the restoration of one's original nature, which is pure, it views human rationality as a hindrance in achieving that pristine state. This is the problem of dualism. The rational mind separates itself from Buddha nature, creating a false identity that keeps it in the state of perpetual ignorance. In his introduction to D. T. Suzuki's book, *Zen Buddhism*, William Barrett makes specific references to this problem as it appears in the western religio-philosophical tradition. He believes that the Hebrews created a division between God and nature, and the Greeks between matter and spirit. This dualism became the center of their religious and philosophical thinking. For the Greeks, rationality became the highest tool to solve the problem created by their dualistic thinking. He writes, "... Plato and Aristotle not only made reason the highest and most valued function, [they] also went so far to make it the very center of our personal identity."[9] Barrett views this as problematic and asserts, "The Orientals never succumbed to this latter error; favoring intuition over reason, they grasped intuitively a center of the personality which held in unity the warring opposites of reason and unreason, intellect and senses, morality and nature."[10] The whole purpose of this discussion is to point out that the dualism created by human rationality has alienated individuals from their true being. It should be pointed out that a critique of reason is also present within the western philosophical tradition; however, the celebration of rationality dominates western culture.

The problem of dualistic thinking is not limited to the western traditions. Within the development of the Zen tradition, there are ample examples that point to this issue. The famous story that involves a poetic competition between the two great Zen thinkers Shen-hsiu (d. 706 C.E.) and Hui-neng (638-713 C.E.) in China is a good example. As the story goes, Hung-jen (601-674 C.E.), the fifth patriarch of Ch'an, was seeking an heir to his patriarchy. He asked for a poem that best described the Ch'an insight. Shen-hsiu, an older learned monk, presented the following stanza:

> This body is the Bodhi-tree
> The soul is like a mirror bright;
> Take heed to keep it always clean,
> And let not dust collect on it.

[9] D. T. Suzuki, *Zen Buddhism* (New York: Doubleday, 1956), p. ix.
[10] *Ibid.*, p. ix.

In response to this, the young monk, Hui-neng, wrote the following:

> The Bodhi tree is not like the tree,
> The mirror bright is nowhere shining;
> As there is nothing from the first,
> Where can the dust itself collect?[11]

Traditionally, these two quatrains have been subjected to various interpretations to bring out various insights of Zen Buddhism. However, one important lesson derived from it concerns the problem of dualism and non-dualism. As D. T. Suzuki points out, Shen-hsiu's poem was rejected on the basis that it posits dualism. On the other hand, Hui-neng became the sixth patriarch on the basis that he clearly understood the non-dual nature of reality that Zen upholds. Suzuki writes, "To see dualism in life is due to confusion of thought; the wise, the enlightened, see into the reality of things unhampered by erroneous ideas."[12]

In the experience of *satori*, there is no rationality. It is an experience in which the *reality* is apprehended as *it* is. It is for this reason that *satori* is spoken of as an "intuitive insight." Lao Tzu understood the import of this experience when he warned against "carving the block," which has been alluded to elsewhere. Likewise, in the Indian philosophical tradition, Shankara warned against the problem of superimposition. In a Chinese fable, this issue has been humorously illustrated. It is said that once a teacher asked his students to draw a picture of a snake in five seconds. One student, who finished the task in three seconds, wondered what he could do to improve his picture. So he added tiny feet to the snake. Obviously, by overdoing it, he distorted the entire picture. Such is the human condi-

[11] *Ibid.*, pp. 67-68.
[12] *Ibid.*, p. 73.

tion. Zen sees us as victims of our own minds.

When Roshi Keido Fukushima advocates, "Be a fool," he is transmitting a Zen insight that has been passed on from generation to generation. To become a fool is to become wise. It is to recognize the limitations of the rational mind, and acknowledge the importance of the intuitive mind. It is accepting that the Buddha nature is always within, and that all individuals can be awakened to it. This insight is beautifully illustrated in a story that has Buddha seated on the Vulture Peak. As the crowd gathered to hear him preach, that day the Buddha simply picked up a flower and spoke no words. Upon seeing this demonstration, Mahakasyapa, one of his disciples, smiled. Evidently he understood the silence of the Buddha, and Zen was born.

"With My Zen Mind"
Calligraphy by Roshi Keido Fukushima

With My Zen Mind

For years I have noticed that whenever Roshi Fukushima writes me a letter, he always signs it with the statement, "With my Zen mind." Every time I read that signature statement, it forces me to examine my own state of mind. I cannot help but focus on my "contaminated mind," overloaded with ego, attachments, and distractions. Once during a family discussion, one of my daughters remarked, "I like you more when you return from Tofukuji." When I probed further, she explained that then I was more agreeable, less prone to losing my temper, and pleasant to be with. Her statement is a constant reminder for me to continue to examine the state of my mind. No wonder the first line of the *Dhammapada* reads, "You are the result of what you have thought."

So what is the state of mind of Roshi Keido Fukushima? When I posed this question to the Zen master, I knew that we had a long discussion at hand. He began by suggesting that perhaps we could focus our conversation on the condition of his mind "before *satori*" and "after *satori*." That seemed to be a good place to start the discussion which was to take us on a long journey of exploration into his Zen life. "I have always tried to follow the Buddhist *dharma*. But before my *satori* experience, now I can say, my life was a life lived with ego. After the *satori* experience, I have no ego. This has brought a new *freedom* in my life." As we probed further, he explained that before *satori* he was attached to *dharma*. The monastic rules seemed difficult, though he believed in them and tried to follow them. However, there was "no joy" in keeping them. They were part of a daily routine. Intellectually he understood their function and the necessity to follow them, but emotionally they brought no satis-

63

faction. After *satori* experience however, everything changed. In his Zen mind, he now feels that he has risen above the dualism of the *dharma*. In order to explain this further, he began to make a distinction between "freedom from" and "freedom to." Before *satori*, there is a tendency to think that one should be "free from" various attachments (including the attachment to the *dharma*). After the *satori* experience, one is "free to" act without attachment and non-attachment. For Roshi Fukushima, this is a new freedom that Zen experience brings. In Japanese Zen, it is explained with the notion of *ji yu*, meaning "to depend on myself." However, this self-dependence is without ego.

The Zen mind is also "spontaneous mind." Before *satori* experience, as the Zen master explains, "The mind is attached to so many things that it loses its ability to act freely in the *present*. That means that the mind is not in its natural state. It is in the defiled state." As it turns out, the master holds that without the Zen experience, people are preoccupied with so many things that they cannot live fully. If we analyze this condition we will discover that most of us either live in the past or in the future. As a consequence, we negate the present. Being in the past means that we worry about the mistakes we have committed that produced our current miserable condition. Living in the future means that we plan ahead for things that will give us joy. Zen wants us to see that the "present" is the real moment. The present is the past of tomorrow and the future of yesterday. So, why not live in the present? I once asked a psychologist what was the secret of joy? "To look for the joy you already have," he responded, "rather than to try to find it in the future." I thought that was a Zen-like answer. It all boils down to the problem of suffering. Living in the past or future is a symptom of anxiety. For Zen, spontaneous mind is an anxiety-free mind.

I told the Zen master that Thich Nhat Hanh, a Vietnamese Zen master, has popularized the phrase, "washing dishes for the sake of washing dishes."[13] What he means by this is that when

---

[13] Thich Nhat Hanh, *The Miracle of Mindfulness* (Boston: Beacon Press, 1975), p. 3.

you are washing dishes, you should be totally there in the present. You should not be washing dishes in order that you may later enjoy a cup of coffee. Through this answer, Thich Nhat Hanh wants to bring into focus the importance of being in the present. I have often asked my students about the cause of their boredom. I think one of the causes of boredom is that we cannot cope with the reality of the present. We want to change our circumstances in order that we may be happy in the future. Boredom is the manifestation of "reality unrelatedness" caused by the negation of the moment. Roshi Keido Fukushima agrees that Thich Nhat Hanh is putting his finger on the Zen understanding of life.

Fukushima explains that in the Zen tradition, the importance of the moment is best described by such statements as, "When I eat, I eat; when I sleep, I sleep." He explicates by stating that when most people eat, they are not totally there. Their minds are elsewhere. Likewise when they sleep, they are not completely committed to sleeping. Their minds are restless. I asked the Zen master what he thought of the people who are often seen reading a book or a magazine while eating a meal. "That's funny," he said. "They can neither enjoy eating nor reading." Sometimes people do that to avoid interacting with their immediate environment because they are too self-conscious. Granted that sometimes reading while eating might be unavoidable, but as a habit it is symptomatic of "moment negation." The Zen master spoke of "mindfulness" as one of the tenets of his Zen mind. As a Buddhist ideal, mindfulness means to be fully aware of every moment of your existence. A mind which is preoccupied with many attachments cannot be "totally there." As a Zen master, Keido Fukushima is mindful of every moment of his life. "I enjoy my day to the fullest," he says, "because I am fully aware from the moment I get up until I go to sleep." How does he cope with distractions, I probed? With a laugh he responded, "I am fully aware of the distractions."

In March 2002, the Roshi visited the College of Wooster for a series of lectures and a meditation session. I asked him to come to my house to have a look at a Zen rock garden that some of my students and I had constructed in my backyard. He was delighted to come and said, "I should give a name to your garden." As the students gathered, Keido Fukushima observed the garden, made some suggestions for improvement, and then proclaimed that he had a name for the garden. We anxiously awaited his announcement. The name he gave was "The Zen Mind." We talked about the symbolism of the rocks, the pine trees, and the gravel associated with the garden. We also discussed the meaning of the ripples created in the gravel by drawing circles around one rock. This was a perfect artistic manifestation of the state of the mind. When a thought enters our consciousness, it creates circles of ripples as the mind tries to deal with it. It is like throwing a pebble in a pond. It creates multiple circles which ultimately dissipate and the water returns to its original calm. In Zen, the state of mind is like that. One can purify the consciousness through meditation, or leave it to create ripple after ripple. The Zen mind is a stable mind. It is a peaceful mind. It is an unperturbed mind. It is an enlightened mind. This is the mind that the Buddhist tradition affirms the Buddha had. Since a Zen master is a living Buddha, Keido Fukushima possesses such a mind as manifested through his behavior.

I once asked the Roshi if his mind was like the mind of a *yogi* in the Hindu tradition. As we began talking, I mentioned to him that in *Sankhya-yoga*, the mind was classified in a variety of ways. It spoke of (1) forgetful mind, (2) distracted mind, (3) occasionally steady mind, and (4) concentrated mind.[14] The goal in *yoga* is to develop a concentrated mind which leads to the experience of *samadhi* (union with Reality). The Zen master responded by saying that he did not know the Hindu tradition that well, but the way *yoga* described the classification of the

---

[14] Mircea Eliade, *Yoga: Immortality and Freedom* (Princeton: Princeton University Press, 1958), ch. 2.

mind made sense to him. I wondered if the *samadhi* experience was similar to that of *satori*. I concluded that these two experiences may be similar, but not the same. In the Hindu tradition, reality is spoken of as Brahman, which can manifest as a personal deity like Krishna. In Zen, there is no such deity. Thus the experience of *satori* is explained as the experience of *shunyata* (emptiness). The Roshi felt that while it was all right to engage in academic discussions, what was essential was the experience. If the Hindu tradition recognized the necessity of the purification of the mind (which it does), then it was based on some *yogi's* experiences. For the Zen master, this is the key. He did not know if his experience of *satori* was like the *yogi's* experience of *samadhi*. It did not matter. What mattered was the kind of life both the *yogis* and the Zen masters lived. He did want to know if the *yogis* perceived the world as *maya* (temporary reality) and wanted to escape from it. As for him, the Zen mind was a fully engaged mind.

The Zen master asked me if I knew of the famous cow-herding pictures.[15] I had used these pictures in my class on Zen to illustrate a point about the Zen mind. He began to explain the meaning of this famous painting. The painting is a series of frames in which a man is depicted with a bull. In one frame, the bull is out of control and the man has difficulty taming it. In another frame, the man is able to catch the bull by its horns and tries to subdue it. Through a series of encounters with the bull, finally the man is able to tame the bull and ride it. As to be expected, the bull is the symbol for the mind. The painting shows the difficulty of taming the mind, bringing it under one's control, and finally experiencing the tranquility of repose.

Keido Fukushima pointed out the difficulties involved in taming his own mind when he was in the monastery. We have already discussed his attachment to his rational mind that led

---

[15] Paul Reps, *Zen Flesh, Zen Bones* (New York: Doubleday, 1961), pp. 136-150.

his guru to ask him to "become a fool." He talked about how, during the meditation, his mind would wander. Sometimes he would hear the sound of a train and could not keep it out of his mind. He wanted to board the train and return home, leaving the monastery behind. He mentioned how in the Chinese and Japanese traditions, the mind is compared to a monkey; it wants to constantly jump from one tree to another. He knows what his training monks are going through as they practice the Zen discipline. He also knows that purifying the mind through hard practice is an absolute necessity for a meaningful Zen life.

Roshi Keido Fukushima classifies the Zen mind into two categories: shallow and deep. Once, our conversation involved a discussion regarding certain Zen priests and Zen masters who had succumbed to temptations, which had created public scandals. We talked about how no religious tradition was free from such problems. As long as the religious leaders are human, they are subject to human frailties. I asked the Roshi how that was possible in Zen, since the Zen master is supposed to rise above ordinary consciousness. He answered by saying that the Zen mind can remain shallow if one does not continue to grow in Zen experience. Does that mean that even a Zen master, after the *satori* experience, can fall from grace? "Yes," said the Zen master, "if the *satori* experience is not sustained by constant practice, one can lose it." He then began to reflect on the "deep" Zen mind. He believes that a Zen master must deepen his Zen mind by constant practice. He regrets that some Zen sects are shortening the Zen training for priests because they need to place them in various temples that are without priests. This is also true in the case of appointing a Zen master. In the Rinzai sect, it is expected that after completing the *koan* study, a monk will spend twenty years in further training. Fukushima believes that if this training is shortened, it will produce "incomplete" masters. Such Zen masters have "shallow" Zen mind. He is satisfied that since taking charge of Tofukuji as the Zen master and the head abbot, he has trained priests with "deep" Zen mind. So far none of them have succumbed to temptations involving sex or money. Speaking of his own Zen mind, he remarks, "I still practice hard."

In Japanese Zen, the heart of Zen is described as *mushin*. This word is usually translated as "no-mind" or "empty mind." For Keido Fukushima, such translations are misleading. He repeats the incident when Prince Charles visited Tofukuji in 1986. Seeing some monks practicing, the Prince had remarked that they were emptying their minds. At that occasion, the Zen master told Charles that Zen believed in *mushin*. He further explicated that *mushin* (no-mind) actually meant "free mind, fresh mind, and creative mind." Through such an understanding, Roshi Fukushima wants to emphasize the positive side of Zen mind. By calling it a fresh and creative mind, he wants to explain that the Zen mind is fully engaged in the world's activities. His own life is a good example of such a mind. Through his involvement in keeping Zen alive, both in the East and the West (his tours in China and the United States), he keeps incredibly busy with his sect's affairs, training monks, doing calligraphy, meeting visitors, and giving numerous lectures and talks. When I asked him about his hectic schedule, he responded by saying, "Zen is not simply about *zazen*. All of life is meditation." One day I inquired in the monastery if I could see the Roshi. I was told that he was at a local pottery shop, individually adorning 3,000 ceramic cups before they could be fired. What had started as a small project had become a huge one. Since these cups with his calligraphy of *mu* (no-ego) were to go to different friends, he made sure that this job was done well.

Zen mind is a simple mind. In this mind, there is a childlike innocence. In India there is a saying which goes something like this: the deeper the river, the less noise it makes; the shallower the stream, the more noise it makes. What is suggested here is that a person of depth has a certain quiet innocence about him/her. On the other hand, a shallow personality is more *childish* than *childlike*. From where does this simplicity stem? Religiously speaking, when people encounter something other than themselves, they stand in awe and wonder in the presence of something higher and beyond. Zen simplicity is a consequence of encountering the Buddha nature. As D. T. Suzuki has pointed out, the experience of *satori* brings a certain sense of passivity and the sense of the Beyond.[16] The sense of humility, simplicity, and childlikeness are manifestations of a deep encounter with the Real. With the loss of ego, one becomes a conduit of peace and tranquility. When I first met the Zen master as a monk in Claremont, I discovered that he was different from others. At that time I did not connect his childlikeness with Zen. Most recently, having observed him as a Roshi and spent time with him, I am convinced that his simplicity goes beyond being a personality trait. It is connected with his religious experience. It is difficult to describe this behavior in words, but I will try. Once during his lecture session, a student asked him how he used his *nyoi* (small Zen stick). The Zen master demonstrated by hitting his assistant. Later on that evening while we were riding together in my car, he burst out laughing and yelled, "Today I am happy because I got to hit my assistant with my *nyoi*." One would not expect a religious heavyweight to express his emotions in such a manner. However, for Keido Fukushima, it seemed a fitting and innocent thing to do. Zen literature is full of stories of Zen masters depicting unusual behavior. Their acts of spontaneity are expressions of their Zen mind.

The Zen mind is full of joy. Several of my students who have had some encounters with Keido Fukushima have commented to me: "He is full of joy. He is so happy. He seems genuine and peaceful." I then ask a rhetorical question, "Why are not we as joyful as he is?" A strange silence pervades the classroom until someone dares to say, "He is enlightened, and we are not." Needless to say, this presents an excellent opportunity for a meaningful discussion on the nature of Zen life. Zen joy is not a manifestation of being funny by telling jokes (although Roshi Fukushima is good at telling jokes also). It is a manifestation of

[16] D. T. Suzuki, *ibid.*, pp. 103-106.

a deep contentment, which comes from encountering the Real. It is acceptance of life as perceived beyond all dualism. More than once I have heard Roshi Keido Fukushima say, "My life is full of joy." I have concluded that he is joyful because his mind is at peace. Having quenched his cravings, extinguished his ego, and relinquished attachments, he is able to transcend the psychological suffering that torments an average person. I once asked him, "Do you ever suffer from physical pain?" With a laugh he responded, "Of course, but for me every day is a fine day." For the Zen mind, joy can be experienced despite pain.

Zen mind is a compassionate mind. It is well known that Buddhism strongly emphasizes *metta* (love) and *karuna* (compassion). Buddha taught that compassion should be exercised towards all beings, not just human beings. As a teaching, it is marvelous, but how does it function in one's life? In Zen, *karuna* is almost a physiological experience. Keido Fukushima explains it in the following manner. During the Zen training, the monks are encouraged to become *mu* (no-self). Of course, becoming *mu* involves transcending the ego. When the ego is gone, the vacuum that is created is automatically filled with compassion. I call it a physiological experience because it appears that the Zen monk *feels* the compassion naturally. He does not try to practice compassion; he cannot help but be compassionate. It is as if the Real is compassionate, and the taste of the Real is the taste of compassion.

During my stay at Tofukuji, I had many opportunities to converse with the resident monks. Once when I asked a monk to describe his feelings for the Zen master, he simply stated, "He is compassionate." When I persisted that, during the *koan* study, the master seemed quite stern and sometimes annoyed, I was told that this was "one sign of his compassion." There seems to be an intricate bond between the training monks and Keido Fukushima. The foreign visitors who have spent some time at Tofukuji also testify to his loving and compassionate nature. His work in China and the United States is an expression of his deep love for suffering humanity. As an embodiment of *karuna*, he has touched many lives.

"Watch, Touch, and Bite"
Calligraphy by Roshi Keido Fukushima

Watch, Touch, and Bite

As a young monk, while training at Hofukuji under Roshi Okada, Keido Fukushima had an experience which he is fond of narrating. One day while burning wood to heat the water for the Roshi's bath, Roshi Okada found him studying a textbook. Keido told the Roshi that he was studying for a chemistry exam. "Is that so?" said Roshi Okada, "Then I will give you a problem to solve. How can you tell the difference between three white powders—salt, sugar, and (Keido has forgotten the third element)?" Having given him the problem, the Roshi went off to his bath. Keido recalls, "I struggled to solve the problem for a long time without any result." That evening the Roshi confronted Keido and asked if he had been able to solve the problem. When Keido replied in the negative, Okada said, "It is very simple; you taste them." Reflecting on this incident, Keido Fukushima feels that he had been looking for a scientific answer while his master gave him the Zen answer. He concludes, "One has to taste Zen."

Nowadays Roshi Fukushima is fond of doing a piece of Zen calligraphy in English to surprise his audiences. One such calligraphy reads "Watch, Touch, and Bite." Often students burst into laughter when suddenly they are shown a work in English in the midst of Chinese and Japanese phrases. When the laughter subsides, the Zen master seizes the opportunity to reflect on the meaning of his work, which is often the last piece. This is his invitation to his audiences to watch Zen, touch Zen, and bite Zen. I am convinced that his experience at Hofukuji of being told to taste the powders to tell their properties has inspired him to teach Zen in this manner.

Why an invitation to Zen? Soon after the terrorists' attack in the United States on September 11, 2001, I spent a long evening with Roshi Fukushima in his quarters at Tofukuji. Having regretted over the chain of events, he began reflecting on the need for spirituality in the modern world. The discussion centered on world crises in all walks of life. He feels that all of humanity is ailing from a "sickness of the soul." Despite material progress and advances in science and technology, there seems to be something missing. We discussed how many social scientists, philosophers, and theologians alike have pointed out the nature of the crises. The Zen master showed a particular concern for the modern youth. He feels that many lack a sense of belonging and are searching for a sense of meaning in their lives. They seem to be alienated from themselves and society. The disillusioned youth are turning to drugs, sex, and violence. Some have given up hope and are living meaningless lives. Many have turned against organized religion and have joined various cults and therapy groups. We used to think that these problems only existed in the West, but they equally engulf the East. The threat of nuclear and chemical warfare seems real. What is humanity to do? Can Zen provide some help? Our conversation turned towards his calligraphy: watch, touch, and bite.

What does he mean by *watch*? To watch is to observe and understand the Zen worldview. We are invited to study Zen, to comprehend its claims, and evaluate its message. The master explains, "Zen begins by asking the basic question, Who are you? It wants to define the self and focuses on the individual, not God." However, focusing on the individual does not mean that it promotes individualism in the sense of "doing one's own thing." The Roshi often critiques the Western emphasis on the individual as the center of reality. He recognizes that the eastern understanding of the self opposes the Cartesian dictum of "*Cogito ergo sum*" (I think, therefore I exist).[17] In Zen, the indi-

---

[17] William S. Sahakian, *Outline—History of Philosophy* (Barnes and Noble, 1968), p. 136.

vidual stands in relation to others as well as in relation to the transcendental reality. Thomas Merton understood this view when he quoted, "No man is an island." The Japanese term, *jiri-ki* (self effort), is used to emphasize that in Zen the burden of enlightenment is on one's self-effort rather than on another power (*tariki*). However, self-reliance does not mean the denial of the experience of a transcendental reality. *Satori* can be explained as the Other, the Real, and the Supreme. But it is not a supreme being in the sense of a Judeo-Christian and Islamic God with a personal identity.

For Zen, an individual is the locus of Buddha nature. When Zen claims that the Buddha nature is "within you," it affirms that the individual is primarily a spiritual being. An individual is essentially a potential Buddha. If such is the case, then why do we not all realize this truth? This is due to *avidya* (ignorance), which has already been discussed in another context. Believing that the Buddha nature is within, Zen excludes the concept of sin as central to the human condition. For Zen, human nature is basically good, but prone to evil due to an unenlightened state. Years ago when I was taking a walk with Gensho (when the Zen master was still a monk) in Claremont, we passed by a park where many children were playing. He remarked, "See the little Buddhas. How wonderful they are." As a student of Buddhism, I quipped, "Shouldn't we call them little *bodhisattvas*?" He responded, "You can, but potentially they are all Buddhas, boys and girls alike." What was striking about this conversation was that it exhibited his sense of compassion.

Within the Zen worldview, having understood the nature of the self, we are invited to examine our own egos, desires, and cravings. I need not repeat what has already been said in this regard in previous chapters. The Zen master, like essential Buddhism, links our own cravings (due to ego) to the problem of suffering. However, he is quick to point out that Buddhism is not a religion of suffering; it is a religion that shows a way out of suffering. Furthermore, it is misleading to think that Buddhism, based on the first Noble Truth of the Buddha, asserts that "life is suffering." Keido Fukushima reports that at American universities and colleges he is often asked why it is that Buddhism focuses on suffering. Why not focus on joy? He explains that Buddhism should be understood as saying that "there is suffering in life" rather than "life is suffering." The term *dukkha* (generally translated in books as suffering) really conveys the meaning of "dislocation." It is as if one had dislocated his/her shoulder. One can still function to some extent in this condition, but with the realization that something is drastically wrong that needs fixing. When I am dealing with the issue of suffering in my Asian Religion classes, some students are apt to point out that all suffering cannot be relegated to human cravings. What about accidents, natural disasters, viruses, etc.? I have talked to some Buddhists who would link all forms of suffering to one's *karma*. However, it needs to be pointed out that if the Buddha wanted to deal with physical suffering, he would have gone to the medical schools of the time. Rather, he chose to become a physician of the soul. Once I asked the Roshi if he sent his monks to the hospital when they needed some medical attention. "Of course," he said, "whatever the cause of physical suffering [*karma* or otherwise], medical help is fine. They also meditate and chant."

In the Zen worldview *satori* is the heart of Zen. However *satori* is often not the focus of discussion in Zen monasteries. The focus is on Zen discipline. The Zen master is disturbed over the fact that in the West the young people are sometimes attracted to Zen because it appears to be mystical. Furthermore, its emphasis on freedom, lack of dogma about God, and a critique of the rational mind, appeals to them. He explains that there is nothing mystical in Zen. It is mystical for those who stand outside the tradition looking in. Within Zen, the Zen experience is an ordinary everyday experience. It is a kind of existentialism but not with a sense of dread and meaninglessness. Zen existentialists take life seriously and embrace the present with one important distinction. It is not living *for the present*, but living *in the present*. The freedom it offers is not in the sense of "doing whatever you want," but "wanting to do" whatever is required for enlightenment. Its critique of rationalism is not anti-intellectualism, but an invitation to experience a supra-rational state of mind.

Zen is not an exclusive property of Buddhism. It cuts across all denominational labels. "One can be a Christian, Hindu, or Muslim and still practice Zen life," says Roshi Keido Fukushima. While many religious claims to universality still want to maintain their uniqueness, Zen makes no such claim. Indeed it has its own history, philosophical bases, and traditions, but the religious experience it speaks of is common to all humanity. One way to explain this feature is to suggest that Zen offers a "method of being religious," rather than a "religion of methods." The Zen master upholds the possibility of "Christian Zen, Hindu Zen, and Muslim Zen." To this date, followers of many faiths have visited the Tofukuji monastery. Among his disciples are believers of many faiths.

What does he mean by *touch*? It is an invitation to get intimate with Zen. During his college tours in the United States, Keido often ends his talks by extending an invitation to the audience to come to his monastery in Japan. Some of my own students have visited Tofukuji over the years. However they soon discover that the life at the monastery is not easy. The Zen master and I have often discussed western students' romantic notions about Zen. Their disenchantment with their own culture has made them turn to many eastern religions. Often they have a naive notion that a little bit of flirtation with meditation and dabbling in the Zen arts, like flower arrangement and the tea ceremony, will bring them peace. D. T. Suzuki was aware of this problem when he asked Roshi Shibayama to impart "true Zen" in the West. Keido Fukushima stands in this tradition. He wants the young people to "touch" Zen through a serious practice. Of course, everyone cannot make a trip to Japan. For them he recommends a serious intellectual investigation of Zen followed by a practice. For those who can visit his monastery, he introduces them to the rigorous monastic life.

For Keido Fukushima, Zen begins with *zazen* (sitting meditation). Touching Zen means to be sincere in sitting meditation every day. At Tofukuji, lay people are allowed to join the monks in evening meditation sessions. They can even join the night sitting. When I asked the Roshi if the presence of lay people might disturb the monks' training, he responded by saying, "No! It is good exposure for them, especially if foreign lay people join in the meditation sessions." I further probed if having women joining in the *sesshin* might not be distracting. Again, he felt that the monks would not be distracted since they were learning to transcend the sexual dualism. He stated, "For monks, men and women are equal. Also, they know that in America they are treated equally." One of the great advantages of practicing *zazen* with the monks is that one gets to see the severe discipline that they maintain. While lay followers are permitted to adjust their posture and take frequent breaks, the monks are required to sit for as long as an hour at a stretch. Not only that, they are often subjected to the Zen stick. The discipline of Zen is carried outside the meditation hall to the dining hall and chanting hall. Furthermore, the monks are expected to observe silence most of the time, whether working, eating, or sleeping. Any romantic notions about Zen are soon dispelled when one observes the monastic life. Touching Zen in the true sense, then, goes far beyond them wearing a few beads, sitting cross-legged, and chanting a few oriental phrases. The Zen master wants his visitors to experience the true Zen.

The Rinzai sect of Zen upholds the strict discipline of *koan* study. Keido Fukushima Roshi does not easily permit the lay visitors to undertake a plan of *koan* study with him. Generally, if the visitor is serious about Zen life and participates in the daily life of the monastery for a sustained period of time, a *koan* study and participation in *dokusan* is possible. He is critical of those Zen masters in the West who have made the *koan* study easy. He once told me how amazed he was to learn that a particular Zen master in American was conducting a *koan* study for a disciple on the telephone. This kind of practice of "dial-a-*koan*" trivializes the significance of *koan* study. For the Zen master, true *koan* study establishes a bond between the master and the disciple. It is only through a close relationship that the master can watch the spiritual progress of the disciple. While we were discussing the "dial-a-*koan*" problem, Keido remarked, "Perhaps soon some people will be studying *koan* through the internet. That is a problem." I share his concern. His invitation to "touch" Zen is to practice it through close contact with an authentic Zen master. It is an invitation to form a relationship with one who exemplifies the spirit of true Zen.

The Zen master is concerned that Zen fascinates many people in the West for the wrong reasons. Many of those reasons, in some way, relate to the problem of self-gratification. This is the problem of ego. As long as Zen is pursued by selfish motives, there is no spiritual progress. The discipline of Zen is centered on mastering the self. There is no better place to observe the process of mastering the self than a Zen monastery. The Zen master wonders why many Zen scholars, when describing the process of Zen life, stop with *satori*. Even D. T. Suzuki has written, "At all events there is no Zen without *satori*, which is indeed the Alpha and Omega of Zen Buddhism." As I talk with Roshi Fukushima, I discover that for him the Alpha and Omega of Zen is compassion. "Touching" Zen for him ultimately means to be compassionate towards all things, human and non-human. This is what Buddhism proclaims as "cultivation of social emotions."

The third component of his calligraphy is *bite*. This is an invitation to taste the fruits of Zen. In a Hindu classic, the *Bhagavadgita*, Lord Krishna instructs Arjuna to renounce all attachments that hinder the taste of salvation, and then to enjoy. It is in this spirit that the Zen master Keido Fukushima invites his audience to taste and enjoy the benefits of Zen. When his American audiences first see him write, "Watch, touch, and bite," they burst into laughter. They are reminded, "Zen is like a slice of a sweet pie. One has to bite it to enjoy it." It is hard to stop after one bite. One ends up eating the whole slice. So it is with Zen. Once you bite into it, if you like it, you want more.

The enjoyment comes in the form of personal freedom. It is the freedom to live in the present without suffering.

Students often remark that the Zen life sounds very peaceful and inviting, but that they do not have the time to spend long hours in meditation. They have academic as well as other responsibilities. The Zen master agrees, but assures them that a little bit of effort made in good faith will go a long way. It will add quality to their life and give them contentment. Zen practice does not require one to join a monastery; but it does require a consistent meditative practice to experience the purification of the mind. The master reminds the students that they are in the business of enlightening their minds through education. However, without a Zen attitude, the mind is contaminated and defiled, resulting in confusion and mental disturbance.

I once quoted a verse from the Christian scriptures to the Zen master which read, "Seek ye first the kingdom of God; all things will be added unto you." I wanted to know if this verse revealed the Zen insight. The master agreed and reiterated that Zen was not confined to Buddhism.

Keido Fukushima's calligraphy, "Watch, touch, and bite," is a welcoming gesture to entice his audience to seek a loving relationship with Zen. He does not hesitate to share his own life's experiences and tell others how Zen came into his life and turned it upside down. He entered the monastery as a *bodhisattva* and became a living Buddha. He wants to take the message of Zen to others in the hope that they too will benefit from it.

The Humor
of the
Zen Master

The famed bridge Tsuten-kyo at Tofukuji

ver the years I have been haunted by the thought—why do I gravitate toward Keido Fukushima's personality? Yes, he has taught me much about Zen. Yes, I have experienced his compassion. Indeed, he has been extremely benevolent toward my students. But the answer lies elsewhere. I have come to recognize that it is his infectious smile and ever-present sense of humor that is so attractive to me. In his company one cannot help but laugh and enjoy the moment. He seems to touch one's heart and unleash the joy that often lies suppressed in one's being. To be in his presence is refreshing and therapeutic. He is indeed the laughing Buddha of Tofukuji.

Despite the Roshi's ever-present sense of humor, his joking and kidding, it would be a mistake to think that the walls of Tofukuji ring with laughter and that there is constant merrymaking among the monks who live there. Tofukuji is a Zen training monastery. As such it observes strict rules of discipline and maintains an austere mood of harsh training. In the *sodo* (monk's quarters), silence is observed as a cardinal rule. However, in the midst of strict monastic observances, one senses the presence of joy. I think this is the key to understanding Keido Fukushima's sense of humor. As the head abbot of Tofukuji, he is an exemplary model of what Zen humor is all about. It is not about being funny and telling jokes in order to remain lighthearted. It is about exuding a genuine sense of joy as an expression of Zen experience. It is about manifesting a sense of contentment as a living testimony to the conquest of suffering. Surely Sakyamuni Buddha must have smiled at his *nirvana*. It is Buddha's smile that has captivated the East. Indeed, Keido Fukushima likes to tell jokes (even to his monks). He is witty and funny. However, his laughter has a deeper meaning.

There is a lighter side of his humor, but there is also a "heavier" side which expresses Zen. In the following pages I will illustrate a variety of meanings that I have found in the Roshi's humor, which speak both to the lighter and the heavier sides. But first, a word about Zen and humor in general.

The history of Zen Buddhism is replete with humor. Conrad Hyers has written:

> In no other tradition could the entire syndrome of laughter, humor, comedy, and "clowning" be said to be more visible and pronounced than in Zen.... In no other religious movement are its principle record..., its technique for spiritual realization, its art and aesthetic, and its portrayals of the spirit and style of those masters whom one is called to emulate, so intimately intertwined with the comic spirit and perspective.[1]

Several biographies of the legendary Zen masters in China and Japan, Zen stories, paintings, and even some *koans* and *haikus* convey the sense of humor in Zen. It is as if humor is an ever-present medium to convey the insights of Zen. There is that famous story that once, while seated on the vulture peak ready to give a sermon, Gautama the Buddha, instead of giving a discourse, held up a flower. Upon witnessing this gesture, one disciple, Mahakasyapa smiled. Earlier in this book I have already given a theological interpretation of this incident. Here it is sufficient to point out that Zen attributes the beginnings of its religious tradition to a *smile*. Needless to say that ever since that signature smile in India, there have been thousands of smiles, laughter, clowning, joking, and so much religious buffoonery in Zen that Conrad Hyers has labeled it the "comic spirit" of Zen.[2]

---

[1] Conrad Hyers, *The Laughing Buddha: Zen and the Comic Spirit* (Wolfeboro, N.H.: Longwood Academic, 1989), pp. 14-15.

[2] *Ibid.*, p. 18.

No monk in the Zen tradition is as famous as the legendary Chinese monk, Pu-tai, who supposedly lived in 10th century China. Today his potbellied images are sold in many gift stores in Asia and adorn the entrances of Chinese restaurants. Popularly recognized as the "laughing Buddha," Pu-tai's image is much different to the image of the historical Buddha, who is believed to have fasted so long prior to his *nirvana* that his ribcage is shown. Equally famous is the towering figure of Bodhidharma, who in contrast to Pu-tai, forever sits gazing at a wall in deep meditation. The tradition has it that Bodhidharma meditated so hard that his legs fell off. While Bodhidharma invokes a response of seriousness, Pu-tai, on the other hand, invites a smile, if not laughter. His exuberant joy and laughter connect him with the Maitreya *bodhisattva*, the Buddha of the future. He becomes a symbol of hope, contentment, joy, and celestial happiness for millions of Mahayana Buddhists, including Zen.

A well-known figure in Japan is Ryokan (1758-1831 C.E.), a wandering monk who frolicked with the children and danced with the villagers. A famous incident has him playing hide-and-seek with the children and getting lost in a haystack only to be found the next day. He is also known for his eccentric behavior to the extent of sheltering lice in his robe.[3] There are many other stories that are told of Zen masters and monks alike bursting into laughter when asked about their experience of *satori*. There are Han-shan and Shih-te (7th century C.E.), "with their boisterous, almost mad, and seemingly near-demonic laughter.... And there are three laughing sages of Hu-hsi, overcome with mirth in every painting, as if a Zen trinity were enjoying some eternal joke."[4] There is a famous story of a Zen monk asking his master, "What is the meaning of Bodhidharma's coming from the West?" The master supposedly asked his monk disciple

---

[3] *Ibid.*, p. 27.
[4] *Ibid.*, p. 26.

to prostrate before him in respect before he would answer his question. As the disciple attempted to bow, he received a strong kick at his derriere by the master. This caused him to have a *satori* experience. As the story goes, after this encounter of being kicked, he said to everyone he met, "Since I received that kick from Ma-tsu [709 - 788 C.E.], I haven't been able to stop laughing."[5]

It is reported that Hakuin (1686 - 1769 C.E.) was fond of telling his students about a certain woman who had a deep understanding of Zen. Wanting to find out for themselves, many of the students would visit the said woman's tea shop. As the story goes, if the students came to her to drink tea, she would serve them with grace and honor. However, if they came to test her Zen experience, she would invite them in the back room of the tea house and strike them with a fire poker. The majority could not escape her beatings.[6] Needless to say that the Zen master Hakuin deliberately tempted his students to seek the woman with the tea shop and be subjected to her unusual method of teaching about Zen.

Another story features another woman—a nun. Once upon a time there was a nun who in the quest for enlightenment made a statue of a golden Buddha and carried it everywhere she went. She worshiped the statue and burned incense in front of it. In her travels she came to a temple that housed many Buddhas. Unwilling to accept the notion that the incense she burned for her Buddha statute might stray toward other Buddhas, she invented a funnel that would carry the perfumed smoke only to her statue. As fate would have it, this practice blackened the nose of her golden Buddha and made it particularly ugly.[7]

R. H. Blyth in his *Oriental Humor* tells the story of a Ch'an monk in China who decided to die in an unusual way—standing upon his head. It seems that Teng Yinfeng, when about to die,

---

[5] Nancy Wilson Ross, *The World of Zen* (New York: Vintage Books, 1960), p. 183.

[6] *Ibid.*, p. 186.

[7] *Ibid.*, p. 187.

inquired of the people how they had witnessed other monks die. Some had seen monks die sitting or lying down, but none had witnessed a monk dying standing up, certainly not standing upon one's head. Upon hearing this, our monk stood on his head and died. The problem came in how to cremate him in this position. Seeing the dilemma, his sister, a nun, reportedly said, "When you were alive you took no notice of laws and customs, and even now you're dead you are making a nuisance of yourself!" Having said that she pushed the dead body with her finger and he fell to the ground. Thereupon the cremation was completed.[8]

Zen stories have Zen masters slapping, kicking, twisting noses, and beating their disciples. None of the stories end in indignation or revenge. The disciples are depicted as tasting the flavor of Zen and in some cases even reaching enlightenment. The humor is also carried into Zen *koans*. When the Zen master Joshu was asked about the significance of Bodhidharma's coming to the East, he pointed to "the cypress tree in the courtyard." When asked whether a dog had Buddha nature, the same Joshu said, "*mu*," which became the famous *koan* known as "Joshu's *mu*." Whether it is "the sound of one hand clapping" or "what was your face before you were born," at first glance many *koans* foster a smile if not laughter.

Zen paintings are no different. In the world of Zen art, no figure has drawn as much attention from the Zen master artists as the figure of Bodhidharma. With their brush strokes they have painted his eyes, nose, ears, eyebrows, mustache, and beard in a manner that brings a smile to the face of the beholder. Not only Bodhidharma, but also caricatures of monks tearing up a Buddhist *sutra*, burning Buddha statues to warm themselves, and taming a tiger are among a variety of art themes that dominate Zen painting. These works of art invoke a humorous

---

[8] Quoted in Ross, *ibid.*, p. 188.

response. We are forced to smile and laugh but then ponder and reflect.

How are we to understand Zen humor that results in a smile or laughter and solicits a deeper response? I agree with Conrad Hyers when he writes:

> Laughter leads toward the debunking of pride and the deflating of ego. It mocks grasping and clinging, and cools desire. It cuts through ignorance and precipitates insight. It turns hierarchies upside down as a prelude to collapsing them, and overcomes dualities and conflicts by embracing and uniting opposites. The whole intellectual and valuational structure of the discriminating mind is challenged, with a result that is enlightening and liberating.[9]

So, such is the story of humor in the annals of Zen. My intention was not to give an exhaustive treatment of the relationship of humor to Zen, but to set the stage for talking about the humor of Roshi Keido Fukushima.

As a custodian of the Rinzai Zen tradition, Keido Fukushima upholds the legacy of those Zen masters who trace their lineage in the antiquity. As such he is the bearer of a Zen torch that will continue to burn for years to come. As to his humor, he stands in the tradition of the "comic spirit" of Zen, but also transcends it. He once told me, "Zen has no humor. It appears humorous to those who live dualistically." But having said that he laughs as if to conceal and yet reveal something deeper about Zen. I shall elaborate on his statement later in this section. First, I wish to illustrate some salient features of Keido's humor as I have come to observe them. Despite his contention that "Zen has no humor," the Roshi is a personification of wit, simplicity, freedom, insight, compassion, transcending dualism, transcending ego, spontaneity, and innocence. In many respects these characteristics are associated with his personality as well as his Zen experience.

[9] Conrad Hyers, *ibid.*, p. 17.

Consider his wit. I recall an incident that occurred when Keido lectured at the College of Wooster. We (his attendant, the interpreter, and I) were waiting in the green room as the audience began to fill the hall. I was a bit anxious since it was my responsibility to introduce him. I was also concerned about the sound system, the microphones, lighting, etc. I turned to Keido and said, "On the stage we have two mikes, one for you and one for your interpreter." Without a moment of hesitation he retorted, "But I need three mikes." Three mikes, I thought, how am I going to get a third mike at this last minute? I turned to the Roshi and in exasperation said, "Three mikes! When I checked with you earlier you said two mikes and that's all we have." With a straight face he said, "Three mikes. I need three mikes." There was a minute left until his talk; the house was packed; and I panicked. Sensing my dilemma, he smiled and said, "Ishwar-san, I need a mike for myself, a mike for my interpreter, and then I need Mike [the name of his interpreter]. I need three mikes." We had a hearty laugh. His assistant opened the door, and we walked on the stage. I sighed with a sense of relief. After my introduction, the Zen master began his talk in Japanese, apologizing for his broken English as his interpreter began translating in English. No sooner than his talk was underway, he burst into perfect English stating, "Tonight I will speak in English and my translator will translate in Japanese for you." After a moment of silence he added, "I am only kidding." Mike was relieved, the audience began laughing, and the lecture went on in Japanese. He had the students' attention.

Once during his calligraphy lecture demonstration, a student asked him, "Roshi, at your monastery in Kyoto, how do you prepare yourself for doing the vast number of pieces that you say you do?" While answering he began telling his audience about the monastery, the room, preparation of the ink, laying of the scrolls, etc. "Sometimes I also hum and sing softly," he said and proceeded to tell an incident. Evidently the monks at the monastery know that their head abbot likes to sing Japanese tunes as he does his calligraphy. They often compliment him on his ability to sing. One day, said the Zen master, a monk complimented him on his singing but then proceeded to ask, "Roshi, what were you singing today? I did not recognize the tune." Keido turned to the audience and spoke in a soft voice, "I was humming the Star Spangled Banner." His audience burst into laughter, and Keido turned back to his calligraphy. After the presentation was over, in the hallway I overheard a conversation about Keido's lecture. Someone was saying, "He is funny. He is witty. Are all Zen masters like him?"

Roshi Fukushima's sense of humor also reflects his sense of freedom. As indicated earlier this freedom is not in the sense of "freedom from," but rather "freedom to." I find this quite refreshing and exemplary of Zen behavior. Let me explain by citing a few instances that I have observed in the Roshi's life.

The reader will recall that I have spent several months at Tofukuji over the past few years. During my stay there I was treated to several formal meals with the Zen master. Sometimes we shared the meal with other guests, but it was often just the two of us. On these occasions the Roshi seldom ate much, but made sure that the guests were treated well. During these meals, the guests were served *saki* as well as beer. Once while I was being served some beer, I put my hand over the glass and said, "I am living in a monastery; I cannot drink. Please do not pour for me." The monk server stopped. The Roshi immediately retorted, "I am a monk, please pour me some." At this the monk poured a very small amount of beer in the Roshi's glass, which he proceeded to drink. We had a good laugh. This spontaneous act taught me a lesson on Zen freedom. Keido Fukushima does not drink; neither is he fond of alcohol. However, he was illustrating his freedom to transcend the monastic vows. I am reminded of a lecture that Professor Donald Lopez, one of the leading authorities of Tibetan Buddhism in America, gave on "Religion of the Dalai Lama" at the College of Wooster campus in April 2003. During the lecture he explained how the Dalai Lama has to meditate every day on the vows of a bodhisattva. Among the vows is one which requires the Dalai Lama to meditate on "the breaking of the vow." Such is the Buddhist sense of freedom.

Roshi Keido Fukushima told me of an incident that further illustrates his sense of humor as well as his sense of freedom. Once when he was scheduled to lecture at Xavier University in Cincinnati, Ohio, it snowed quite heavily and his host could not reach the auditorium in time to introduce the Roshi. However, the Roshi had made it to the lecture hall and so had a sizeable crowd. He reports that everyone silently waited for the arrival of the host. Eventually, the Roshi broke the silence and suggested that they sing some songs. The audience started with "Row, row, row your boat, gently down the stream," then asked the Roshi to sing something in Japanese. He obliged by singing, "Sakura, Sakura ..." When he was finished, a lady began singing with a beautiful voice, "You are my sunshine, my only sunshine." She sang so beautifully that the audience became extremely quiet and listened to her. The song ended with a pin-drop silence in the hall. The Roshi got up, looked at the lady, rubbed his bald head two or three times and showing it to the lady said, "*I am your sunshine.*" The hall roared with laughter. Just then the host entered the hall in the midst of a standing ovation and wondered what had happened.

In March 2003 I visited the Roshi in Cincinnati, Ohio where he was scheduled to give yet another lecture at Xavier University. On the dresser in his room there was a framed picture of an American lady that I could not make out from a distance. During our conversation, I found myself periodically glancing at the picture, wanting to know who that might be. Sensing my curiosity, the Roshi asked his attendant monk to bring the picture over to me. As the photograph was being handed to me, he said, "This is my latest attachment," and laughed. I looked at the picture and could not help but chuckle. It was a photo of the singer Joan Baez with her message, something like, "With best wishes to the Zen master," along with her signature. Evidently, one of Roshi's American friends in Cincinnati, knowing how much he likes Baez's music wrote to

Cincinnati, knowing how much he likes Baez's music wrote to her about the Roshi. In response, Joan sent her greetings with a signed self-portrait. The friend had it framed and presented it to the Roshi. The Roshi accepted the portrait with gratitude and displayed it as his "new attachment." The Zen master loves coffee, Godiva chocolate, and old bridges. He is not attached to any of these things but can enjoy them in his freedom.

The Roshi's humor is also reflected in his childlike simplicity and innocence. Once while I was visiting Waseda University in Tokyo, a professor asked me, "Since you are living in a Zen monastery, do you find the monks a bit naive?" To a certain extent, this professor's observation was correct. There is a certain sense of naiveté that pervades among the monks. However, as I tried to explain to the professor, there is a certain "naiveness" that is peculiar to Zen. It is not a negative quality but a positive "naturalness." The Zen master is a highly educated and well-informed individual. However, at times he displays a certain innocence that has a Zen quality. To an outsider such behavior expresses a certain kind of humor.

The Zen master tells of an incident that occurred while he was a training monk under Roshi Okada. Gensho was instructed to be on his best behavior when the monks visited lay people's homes for various ceremonies and rituals. Even then Gensho was known for his smile and friendly personality. He tells the story that he was once invited, along with other monks, to perform certain ceremonies at a house where someone had died. Throughout the ceremony, Gensho kept smiling. Later someone asked, "Who was that smiling monk at the funeral?" As a young monk, Gensho was being himself, natural, spontaneous, and simple. His teacher, Roshi Okada, had to teach him how to behave at funerals. As a Zen master, Keido Fukushima has not lost his sense of being natural and simple. There is a childlike quality about him that is attractive and infectious.

Roshi Fukushima's humor is also expressed in his Zen insight. It is reflected in his appreciation for Zen attitude when he sees it. He once told me an incident that occurred in

Charleston, South Carolina a few years ago, which relates to this point. The Roshi is fond of looking at old bridges. One fine morning he took a walk under a bridge and saw a man fishing. The man had a dog, a transistor radio, and something to drink as he relaxed in his chair, gazing at his fishing pole. He was completely oblivious to a Zen master walking past him in strange-looking clothes. On the way back from his walk, Keido stopped and asked the man, "What are you catching?" "Oh, nothing," answered the man without looking up. "Ah," said the Roshi, "you have fresh air, good music, and a beautiful dog. It seems you are catching everything." At this point, the Zen master says to me: "You know in Zen nothing is everything and everything is nothing. That is the secret of *shunyata* [emptiness]." I nod. He continues to finish the story. Upon hearing Keido's comments about "nothing = everything," the man gave him two thumbs up. The Roshi handed him his business card. Without looking at it, the man put it in his pocket. The Zen master departed. But he had an afterthought that he likes to share with his audience when talking about this man who was catching "nothing" but "everything." He imagines that in the evening when this man returns home, while talking to his wife, he reaches in his pocket and finds the Roshi's card. He looks at it and, realizing that he has had an encounter with a Zen master, gives two thumbs up to his wife. I have often wondered if that man ever did what the Zen master imagined. However, it has made me reflect on the humor and the Zen insight that the Roshi possesses.

He narrated another incident to me that took place in his monastery some time ago. He recalls that often in the monastery kitchen, when the monks cook food, they have to make use of what is made available to them. It seems that for days the monk in charge of the cooking was putting bamboo shoots in the soup. This went on for lunch and dinner for a long time. Finally, the Roshi confronted the cook and demanded in a somewhat raised voice, "Can't you do something different?" The monk nodded and promised that he would try. The evening came, and when the meal was served, once again there were bamboo shoots in the soup. Keido once again confronted the culprit and forcefully chided, "Didn't I ask you to do something different?" With his head bowed, the monk answered, "We did, sir. We cut the shoots *differently*." "Oh! Okay. Then carry on," responded the Zen master. Laughing over the incident, the Roshi looks at me and says, "That was a good Zen answer." Once again when I ponder on this story, I find humor as well as Zen insight in it.

Consider yet another incident. In one of his lectures, the Roshi narrated his encounter at a Chinese shop in San Francisco. It so happened that one year on his trip to the United States, Keido forgot to bring enough rice paper for his calligraphy demonstration. He was deeply concerned, but someone directed him to a shop in Chinatown that might have the paper he needed. Sure enough, an old Chinese man, the shopkeeper, provided him with the paper he needed. The following year Keido forgot to bring enough ink and rushed to the same shop. Again the old man provided him with the ink he needed. However, this time he remarked, "If next year you forget to bring the Zen master, we can sell you that too." There is no particular Zen insight for me in this story, but it is funny. The fact that Keido Fukushima likes to tell this story over and over suggests something about his Zen mind. He found the old man's presence of mind insightful, somewhat like the mind of a Zen person. As for him, after this encounter in San Francisco, he never forgets to bring enough materials for his calligraphy.

Roshi Keido Fukushima's humor is also expressed in his acts of compassion toward his monks. Knowing that the monks are not permitted to laugh in his presence, he sometimes still tells them jokes. The monks listen and control their laughter. When they leave, the Roshi knows that he will hear their laughter after they pass a certain corridor in the hallway. He times them. And sure enough, the monks' laughter is faintly audible as they crack up behind the hidden walls of the monastery. The Roshi is fond of telling his own experiences with his own master, Roshi Okada. Master Okada was fond of telling jokes to his training monks, but he would not permit them to laugh before the punch line. The senior monks would often get the joke ahead of time and start to giggle. The junior monks (including Gensho) would struggle to understand, and would often fail. However, when Master Okada would say, "Now you can laugh," they would laugh. Once Gensho's friend asked him, what was so funny about the joke? Gensho replied, "I don't know." "Why are you laughing so hard then?" asked the friend. "Because the Roshi asked us to laugh," came the reply. Keido recalls his time with Roshi Okada with fond memory and remembers his compassion toward his monks. Perhaps his treatment of his own monks is modeled after his own experiences with Roshi Okada.

Sometimes compassion takes a different form and may not be perceived as very pleasant. Once during his visit to the College of Wooster, a faculty member asked him to explain the purpose of the "Zen stick." He quickly answered, "It is out of compassion that we use the stick." Having said that, he proceeded to tell an incident that occurred at his monastery. He explained that out of many *koan*s used in the Rinzai sect, the answer for two of them requires "the slapping of the Zen master by the training monk." Once during *dokusan* (*koan* interview session), a monk slapped Keido, but it was for a wrong *koan*. Keido picked up his *nyoi* (small Zen stick) and proceeded to strike the monk on his back. Just then the monk turned abruptly and the *nyoi* landed on his head instead, causing it to bleed. Keido dismissed the monk, who left the room in pain. Not knowing what had transpired inside, the next monk to enter the room to have an audience with the Roshi was trembling like a leaf with the fear of receiving the same treatment. The Roshi ended the story by remarking, "You see in the monastery we work very hard together to have the Zen experience." We had a good laugh.

In the preceding pages I have attempted to present Roshi Keido Fukushima's humor as I have observed it. I shall now briefly turn to the master's own understanding of his humor and the place of humor in Zen as he views it.

The Roshi attributes his sense of humor to the influences of Roshi Okada and Roshi Shibayama. However, they were both very different. While Master Okada was light-hearted and easy-going, Shibayama was gentle but serious. While Okada told jokes and laughed openly, Shibayama's humor was subtle and quiet. Keido unconsciously incorporated characteristics of both and integrated them into his personality.

When Gensho was a training monk at Hofukuji, he learned a lot about his teacher, Master Okada. It seems while growing up Okada had difficulty in speaking. In order to master this deficiency he decided to go to a traditional Japanese theatre where comedians told jokes. These jokes are taken from the events of daily life and people connect to them easily. As a poor student, Okada saved money for the comedy theatre. Soon he became addicted to the comedy. Keido remarks, "Master Okada got attached to comedy and forgot about learning how to talk." When Okada became the Zen master at Hofukuji, he would often gather his monks around an old broken down radio and listen to comedy theatre programs. Sometimes he would smack the radio for it to function. He loved the comedy so much that they would listen to the old programs over and over as they were broadcast. The older monks knew the jokes so they would laugh. The younger ones laughed when the master told them to do so, even though the jokes were beyond them.

Roshi Fukushima recalls his association with Roshi Okada with fond memories. "Although he was a strict master, his humor attracted me," recalls Keido. It appears that Master Okada was able to combine light-hearted comedy with his Zen experience. This synthesis, which came to him naturally, made him an attractive Zen master among the lay people as well. Roshi Fukushima recalls how during Okada's visits to various temples, people would love to gather to hear him. Gensho often accompanied his master and found his interaction with the parishioners quite refreshing. Reflecting on Okada's influence on him, the Roshi remarks, "I think in humor I have passed Roshi Okada." When I pushed further, he stated that, "looking back it appears that Master Okada had an old-style humor. I have a new-style humor." What he means is that being a product of his time, with limited travel experience and geographical confinement, Master Okada drew from his experience. On the other hand, Keido Fukushima is a product of a different time. Well-educated, widely traveled, and the author of several books, he is exposed to different people and cultures. Consequently, his experiences are quite different.

Roshi Keido Fukushima credits his second master, Roshi Shibayama, for his humor as well. He remarks: "I always wanted to imitate Roshi Shibayama. There was something deep and profound about his personality." As to Shibayama's humor, it was subtle, penetrating, and refined. "Shibayama hardly told jokes," says Keido, "but his personality made people smile." When I asked Keido to give an example of Shibayama's humor, he responded by saying, "His sarcasm sometimes was his humor." I prompted him by saying, "Ah! I detect a bit of sarcasm in your talks as well. Did you learn that from Roshi Shibayama?" He laughed and said, "Maybe!" Then he added, "Roshi Shibayama had five disciples who were friends [including Gensho]. Among themselves they often agree that I am more like Master Shibayama."

Roshi Fukushima admits that as a young boy his personality was very different. He definitely lacked a sense of humor. The change came gradually as he came in contact with his Zen masters. He believes that although Zen lends itself to humor, one's personality has a lot to do with it. He states: "All Zen masters in Japan do not have a sense of humor. In fact many are very serious and quiet." When I asked him if he was considered to be a funny Zen master in Japan, he laughed and said, "I don't know. Probably my monks don't think so." The fact is that during my stay with his monks, when I asked some of them about the Zen master, they responded that indeed he was a strict Zen master, but with a sense of humor. Some called him "number one" in the monastery, who cared for their well-being.

Recognizing his own sense of humor, and a tradition of humor that permeates the Zen tradition, the Roshi says, "*Zen has no humor.*" I was quite intrigued by this and proceeded to quiz him on his statement. It turns out that for him there is a much deeper and philosophical meaning behind what is perceived to be humorous in Zen. A Zen monk or a Zen master is not funny for the sake of being funny. The humor is an expression of their Zen experience. Of course, some humor is a manifestation of one's personality. As such, it is just that—a manifestation of personality, nothing more. Sometimes the lay people may interpret it as a manifestation of the Zen experience, but that is a mistake. As our conversation continued, Keido reflected further. "Zen has no *humor* just as Zen has no *mysticism*," he stated. In Keido's mind, many people in Japan as well as in the West think of Zen as "mystical" as if there is some hidden secret in it. For him Zen is not mystical, it is "natural." Likewise, humor is a natural expression for those who are within the Zen tradition. For the outsiders, who are devoid of Zen experience, objectively speaking, it appears humorous.

Philosophically speaking, Roshi Fukushima sees humor existing within the realm of *dualism.* Since most lay people exist on this level, they find certain aspects of Zen funny. It is important to realize that the *genesis* of the apparent humor of Zen is elsewhere—it is in the *non-dualistic* realm. That is to say, when a Zen master or a Zen monk acts or utters something which appears to be humorous to us, for him the labels "funny," "humorous," or "absurd" do not apply. They are manifestations of the experience transcending dualism. From this perspective, *Zen is what is.* It is neither sad nor funny. Roshi Keido Fukushima is not against people seeing humor in Zen. However, they should understand it for what it is. He reiterates: "A Zen person laughs when he laughs and weeps when he weeps. That's all!"

During our discussion on humor I asked the Roshi about those Zen masters in China and Japan who told funny stories to their disciples or behaved like the legendary Sufi, the incomparable Mulla Nasrudin.[10] The Roshi agreed and pointed out that such stories or acts can be used as an *upaya* (means) to illustrate a point. However, he pointed out that the purpose behind such activities is to engender Zen experience, not to teach about humor. Furthermore, within the narratives, the Zen person who is the object of humor, does not think of himself as funny. Only the others do. I agree with the Roshi. In the case of the Sufi Mulla Nasrudin, he does not see himself as funny or absurd. He behaves as he sees fit. Furthermore, within the Sufi tradition, his stories are told not to teach about Sufi humor, but about Sufi experience. On this issue I find a remarkable similarity between the Sufi tradition and Zen.

When I spoke to the Roshi about the American interest in Zen, partly due to its mysticism, art, sense of freedom, and humor, he did not think that any of these reasons in themselves was wrong. As for humor, he felt that it was human nature to enjoy a funny story or a joke with a friend. But a serious student of Zen must not be attracted to Zen for the wrong reasons. He pointed to his calligraphy piece in English, "Watch, Touch, and Bite," and said, "I do this piece for the Western audiences to invite them to experience real Zen. Of course, they can begin with their own interest [including humor]."

Many of my discourses with Roshi Fukushima have ended with smiles and laughter as we have reflected on Zen. After our discussion on "Zen has no humor," I am left with a question. When I laugh in his company, I laugh *with* him; but does he sometimes laugh *at* my dualistic mind? If he does, it is in the spirit of Zen. He is the Laughing Buddha of Tofukuji.

---

[10] Within the Sufi Islamic tradition, the legendary figure of Mulla Nasrudin is well known for his "absurdities," which reflect Sufi insights. For details, see Idries Shah, *The Exploits of the Incomparable Mulla Nasrudin* (New York: E.P. Dutton & Co., Inc., 1972).

Roshi Keido Fukushima

Epilogue

Roshi Keido Fukushima is a visionary. His Zen is not confined to the walls of Tofukuji, but has reached the mountains of China and the shores of the United States. Like a *bodhisattva*, he continually vows to perfect himself in Buddhist virtues and extends his compassion toward all humanity.

During many of our conversations, Roshi Fukushima emphasized his own desire to deepen his Zen experience. When I confronted him with the notion that "he is a Zen master, a living Buddha on earth," he insisted that he must continually practice hard to transcend his ego and master his attachments. When I reminded him of certain scandals in Zen monasteries in Japan and Zen centers in the United States related to sexual misconduct or embezzlement, he agreed that these problems existed due to what he calls "weak Zen." Using the Christian theological idiom, he believes that "the Zen master can fall from grace." For him *satori* experience needs to be deepened continually through study, worship, chanting, and meditation. When I compared his thought on this issue with the Christian notion of "maturity in faith," he agreed. He called my attention to one of the *teisho* (a *dharma* talk) he had given at Tofukuji, to which I was invited. He explained that his *teisho* is a confession of his faith before the image of the Buddha. This exercise is a constant reminder for him that he has to "prove himself to the Buddha." He enlightened me by telling me that according to the Buddhist tradition, Sakyamuni Buddha and Bodhidharma are believed to be "still practicing." So must he.

As a visionary, Roshi Fukushima is extremely concerned about the spreading of "weak Zen" in Japan and the United States. He finds it unacceptable that some Zen masters are given license to preach Zen and make disciples when their training is "incomplete." Within the Rinzai tradition, a Zen priest should continue his Zen training for at least ten years after leaving the monastery. After that he must continue to practice another ten years on his own. Subsequently, if he is deemed fit by his Zen master, he could become a master himself. According to Roshi Fukushima, "This is the correct method of training Zen masters." He regrets that some Zen sects are cutting the training period short. Not only that: it bothers him that some Zen masters in the West have devalued the importance of the *koan* study. He was shocked to learn that at least one Zen master was conducting the *koan* studies over the phone.[1] He jokingly says, "Perhaps in the future we will train the Zen masters over the internet." He was particularly disturbed that in Japan there was at least one Zen group that held three-month intensive training for foreigners. If one attended three such sessions, one could be licensed as a Zen master. Needless to say the Roshi does not condone these kinds of developments. It is his aim to rectify this situation by imparting the true Zen tradition. Since coming to Tofukuji, Keido has trained over one hundred monks. He is satisfied that his students are custodians of "complete" Zen. His vision is to continue to make true Zen disciples in the West.

Roshi Shibayama and Fukushima have been appropriately called, "Bridges of Zen."[2] In the legacy of D. T. Suzuki and Shibayama, Keido has largely focused his attention on America for the past twenty years. Roshi Fukushima is extremely fond of old bridges and seizes every opportunity to visit old bridges during his visits to the United States. When I asked him if he saw the "bridge" as an important metaphor for life, he agreed. "We are always crossing over," he says, "to the other shore." But, in crossing over, "we must build *strong* bridges." He has a lot to say about his crossing over to America from Japan and the condition of American Zen as he sees it.

On the positive side, Keido finds a lot of vitality and activity in American Zen. He feels that the evolution of Zen from the 1960s to the 2000s has been progressive. In the beginning ('60s), he feels that Americans were curious about Zen but not serious

---

[1] Keido Fukushima has no personal knowledge of the Zen master who conducts *koan* interviews on the phone. He was told about it by some of his American disciples.

[2] Audrey Seo and Stephen Addiss, *The Art of Twentieth-Century Zen* (Boston: Shambhala, 1998), ch. 7.

about Zen. Now he finds that the situation has changed. There is a genuine interest in learning about Zen spirituality. It is his contention that many Americans "are willing to practice Zen discipline." He realizes that American Zen is "mixed." There are Korean and Tibetan, as well as Japanese, Zen influences in America. The people are free to move in and out of various centers, which he finds quite acceptable. Furthermore, a strong point of American Zen is that "it is a lay movement." It has not created a hierarchy between a professional Zen class and laity as in the East. The Roshi finds this "equality" quite appealing. He states: "In the *Nirvana Sutra* Buddha says that everyone has Buddha nature. Therefore everyone is equal." He is hopeful that American Zen has opportunities for women as well. He observes that in Rinzai Zen in Japan, there are no nunneries. The one and only nunnery in Kyoto was closed in 1980. Supportive of the women's movement for equal rights, Keido appreciates women's interest in Zen in America.

For Roshi Fukushima, the future of American Zen is in the hands of the American youth. His decision to visit over twenty universities and colleges in America every year is based on his affection for young people. He became interested in the youth during his stay at Claremont Graduate School in the 1970s. As I reported earlier, he started the K-C (Kyoto and Claremont) connection, which is now extended to many other colleges. I once asked him if he had visited the various Zen centers in the United States. He replied, "No! The Zen centers have their own Zen masters. I want to work among the college students." He finds the young people inquisitive and curious about Zen spirituality. Over the years he has not only lectured at American colleges, but has invited students to practice Zen at his monastery in Kyoto. Keido feels that young people are somewhat disenchanted with the American way of life and are looking for spiritual nourishment. Their general interest in Eastern religions is an indication that something is missing in their spiritual development.

On the negative side, the Roshi is concerned about the American interest in "instant gratification." He knows that people want a quick fix to their problems. For every ailment they pop a pill. For complicated problems they want fast and easy solutions. He worries that some Zen centers have succumbed to this kind of cultural pressure and are diluting Zen to fit the needs of the people. He states, "There is no *instant Zen*. Zen practice requires discipline, self-control, and hard practice." It also concerns him that in America, religion becomes a commodity, something to use and then throw away. When I shared with him the thought of a Tibetan Buddhist scholar, Chogyam Trungpa, who calls this phenomenon "spiritual materialism," the Roshi agreed.[3] It is his hope that as interest in Zen continues the Americans will come to understand the true spirit of Zen. It is for this reason that he has made it his mission to come to America every year to lecture, teach, and hold meditation sessions. Not only that, he is in the process of preparing his American disciples who will eventually take over his life's work.

Keido is fond of using the term "International Zen" when he speaks of his work in Japan, China, and the United States. When I asked him if International Zen had some specific teachings, principles, or theology, he simply said, "No!" However, it has the participation of youth, laymen, and women. It also fosters a dialogue with other world religions as well as with scientists. The Roshi believes that this is something D. T. Suzuki had started. During his many trips to Europe and America, Suzuki engaged in a dialogue with various philosophers, scientists, and religious leaders. The goal of this dialogue was to nurture mutual understanding and to clarify misunderstandings about Zen. He also believed that Zen could provide spiritual nourishment to western people. D. T. Suzuki also studied Christianity, western philosophy, and psychology. Keido does not claim to have the same breadth of knowledge as D. T. Suzuki. Nonetheless, he is among the few Zen masters who have attended graduate classes. He continues to have dialogue with Christian theologians and scholars of world religions. Therefore, International Zen is not parochial, but universal. When I asked him if he was interested in organiz-

---

[3] See Chogyam Trungpa, *Cutting Through Spiritual Materialism* (Boston: Shambhala, 1987).

ing conferences and bringing scholars together to discuss International Zen, the Zen master showed no interest in such efforts. He simply stated, "That is the task of the intellectuals who are interested in such things. I only want to quietly keep on working and do what I am doing."

Keido's work in China to revive and establish Ch'an (Zen) Buddhism has already been reported earlier (see Prologue). He is extremely excited about helping the Chinese rebuild their old temples and monasteries. As a scholar and Zen master, he feels emotionally connected to both India and China. On one of his trips to China some twenty years ago, he made a point to visit the Ch'an master Joshu's temple. He took a pledge at one of the pagodas associated with Joshu's temple that he would give *dharma* talks on Joshu's *Records*. He told me that it took him seven years to accomplish this task. As far as he knows, Hakuin also accomplished this feat, which not many Zen masters have attempted. In Joshu's *Records* there are 520 stories that have deep Zen insights. Joshu was a master storyteller, and so is Roshi Fukushima.

Almost every year Keido returns to China to observe the progress that the Chinese Buddhists are making to rebuild their temple in the Kin Zan mountains. He is pleased that the Chinese authorities have granted permission to the Chinese people to rebuild this particular temple. He reports that many Chinese Buddhists hold the view that if China is promoting "free economy," it should also promote "freeing religion." The Tofukuji sect of Rinzai Buddhism is committed to helping the Chinese Buddhists of Sei-an City rebuild their old religious site. Keido remains committed to this endeavor and has taken leadership in this mission. It is comforting to him that several Buddhist sects in Japan like Shingon, Tendai, and Soto Zen are helping to rebuild religious institutions in China as well. He is delighted that about five years ago, the Chinese, with the help of the Japanese, were able to rebuild Joshu's temple, which is thriving under the leadership of the resident priest and the Ch'an master, Jo-ei. For Keido, "In China there is enthusiasm for religion now." In the spirit of International Zen, he is happy to be a part of this religious revival in China.

It is Roshi Fukushima's hope that in the future his American disciples will spread the message of Zen in the English-speaking world. The heart of this message is *freedom*. He derives his inspiration from the Zen master Ummon who believed that the task of Zen is to make people "free." For Ummon, Keido believes, "to be free means to experience inner freedom." Reflecting on the human condition in modern times, it is his observation that people (particularly in the West), despite their political, social, and economic freedom, feel trapped. Their loneliness, anger, frustration, tension, lack of happiness, and violence are manifestations of their suffering. Zen experience can free them to a more fulfilled life. As he likes to say, "It is not 'freedom from,' but 'freedom to' live as life is meant to be lived." His message is loud and clear. It may serve us well to ponder on the famous *koan*, "What is your original face before you were born?"

Roshi Keido Fukushima's concerns for the future of Zen parallel some of the concerns of the Vietnamese Zen personality, Thich Nhat Hanh. Keido supports the notion of "engaged Buddhism."[4] It is his vision to make Zen relevant to everyday life. He regrets that in this area Zen is "twenty years behind ... Pure Land Buddhism in Japan." He is appreciative of the social work that these Shin Buddhists have undertaken in Japan. He applauds their work among the underprivileged and the poor in Japanese society. Furthermore, he recognizes that many Shin Buddhist priests are more involved in interfaith dialogue. It is comforting to him that some of the younger Zen priests are becoming more socially conscious. They are supporting social work in the area of education and the medical field. He promotes such efforts among his own former students and disciples. I remember once that during Roshi Shibayama's visit to Claremont, California, I asked him if Zen was "socially conscious." He responded by saying, "In this area we have to learn more from western Christianity." Roshi Shibayama's openness to interfaith dialogue and the need for a progressive Zen survives in

---

[4] For Thich Nhat Hanh, "engaged Buddhism" is based on the Buddhist principle of "mindfulness." It seems to me that it also has social implications.

Keido Fukushima. He is transmitting that legacy to the younger generation.

In addition to Roshi Fukushima's interest in promoting social work and interfaith dialogue, he is keenly interested in ecology and world peace. He once told me, "In Zen, nature comes first, then the Buddha's experience." In his lectures and talks, the Roshi often takes up the problem of the environment. It pains him to see what modernization has done to our air, water, and earth. Japan, he believes, has been as much victimized by ecological disasters as the urban West. He firmly holds that people need to apply Buddhist insights to tackle ecological problems. In his mind, pollution, exploitation of natural resources, and over-consumption are consequences of "bad desires." Recently, I told him that Mahatma Gandhi had once said, "The world has enough for man's need, but not his greed." He stated, "Gandhi was right." How craving leads to suffering is Buddha's primary teaching.

Keido remains committed to world peace. At the time when the terrorists destroyed the World Trade Center in New York, the Roshi was to address a large gathering of lay people who had come to Tofukuji to listen to his *dharma* talk and practice meditation. He opened the meeting with a greeting and then invited his audience to a silent meditation in memory of this tragedy. He encouraged his audience to work for peace and refrain from violence. Later, when I met him to continue our discussion about his life and Zen, he reflected on the American tragedy, which he believed was a tragedy for the whole world. He thought that events like these were caused by "bad ego." He grieved for the innocent people who had lost their lives, but then said, "We have to show compassion even to the people who have bad ego." As we talked, he reiterated that violence was not the way to world peace. The more I listened to him that evening, the more I wondered how much he sounded like the Dalai Lama.

A creative mind—witty and humorous, compassionate and loving, curious and caring—Roshi Keido Fukushima is a progressive Zen master of our time. His Zen is contagious. It is not only transmitted through his teachings, but also through his smile and laughter.

Roshi Keido Fukushima

Appendix: Impressions

During the course of writing this book, it occurred to me that perhaps I should ask some of the Roshi's friends, disciples, and acquaintances to contribute to this volume by giving their brief impressions of him. I am delighted that several individuals, included in this appendix, have agreed to do so.

*

* * *

When Roshi Fukushima accompanied his teacher Roshi Shibayama to California for the first time, he met and befriended the students of the Claremont colleges as Gensho. I was one of those students. Although he had completed his monastic training and was already destined to become a Zen master in his own right, his humble and cheerful spirit suggested a senior monk completely devoted to the needs of his teacher, and an accessible friend attentive to the spiritual struggle of young Americans. Gensho returned to Claremont alone two years later. During that year of personal investigation into American spiritual practice, he expanded his circle of friends to include a small *zazen* group, which he continued to lead as a simple senior monk. Occasionally, his difficult schedule permitted a little vacation time and on one long weekend we visited the Grand Canyon for the first time. That trip to the south rim required a long dusty drive over rolling high desert that afforded no hint of the dramatic terrain ahead. When he stepped from the car and caught his first glimpse of those endless mountains rising from the depths of the canyon, he literally staggered and gripped the railing as if vertigo had suddenly overcome his sense of balance. That night, camped in the northern Arizona desert, he explained his experience. Training monks learn a vast collection of poetic literature that define and refine Zen experience, and one of the phrases frequently used to express the mysterious and overwhelming beauty of the differentiated world as Buddha nature itself, describes layer upon layer of endless mountains. Gensho explained that at that moment he witnessed that T'ang dynasty expression of deep Zen experience not as metaphoric literature, but as a physical manifestation with all the marvel and grandeur of the ancient poetry. For him, every experience deepened his Zen life. After a simple dinner of noodles and soup cooked over a fire he slept comfortably in the back of a Datsun pickup.

> *En Zan Kagi-ri Na Ri*
> *Heki So So*
> (Distant blue-green mountains
> appearing layer after layer.)

In his first year as Roshi Fukushima of Hofukuji, no senior monk helped him guide his American novice monks through the complexities of rural monastery life. When the days arrived for begging in the markets of country towns, he again accepted with good humor and humility the responsibility of personally training his American disciples. Gensho, now Keido, donned the straw hat, sandals, and begging bag of a training monk and led the way from the temple gate down to the railway station. Hours later, on the long walk back up the hill from the station, his gait never slowed despite the cold rain and worn out straw sandals. His good humor trailed tangibly behind him encouraging his monks to make every step a pure act. His devotion to training never wavered. That summer the time came to clean the neglected *takuan* (dried radish) pickle barrels that had been sealed for twenty years. When the lids came off, the pungent aroma overwhelmed everyone except Roshi, who laughed and exclaimed with a big smile, "Good smell"; the same English words he had encouraged us with on the day we learned to take the night soil to the garden. For Roshi, every fragrance, every perception was the experience of pure Zen mind.

Gan ri Ni ri Zetzu
Sho Sha
(Everything I see or hear is pure and clean.)

In his first year as abbot of Tofukuji, Roshi Fukushima presided at the one-year ceremony commemorating the death of Tofukuji's previous *kancho* (abbot). At the altar of the great Buddha hall, the Zen masters of Myoshinji, Daitokuji, Kenninji, Tenryuji, Nanzenji, and Tofukuji chanted for the late abbot. Surrounding them sat more than a hundred other Zen masters, abbots, and priests from monasteries and temples all over Japan. His bearing at that momentous and esoteric ceremony seemed impossibly distant from the cheerful Roshi struggling to re-open a dormant monastery with the help of only three monks. Mysteriously, the same spirit of Zen clearly inhabited the new abbot of Tofukuji who solemnly addressed the Buddha in ornate ceremonial attire, and the young Zen master working beside his monks in rolled up sleeves. Smiling and laughing at tea or fearsome and awe-inspiring at *sanzen*, he remained the same true teacher.

Ichi Mu I
No Shin Nin
(One true person of no degree.)

At a summer *sesshin*, fifteen centuries after Bodhidharma arrived in China, Roshi Fukushima gave *sanzen* for a *zendo* filled with earnest monks and lay disciples. The grandeur of old Tofukuji had been restored and outside the monastery walls, tourists from all over the world strolled through its magnificent gardens. Inside the monastery walls another bridge from Tofukuji to the rest of the world was forming. The line for *sanzen* was no longer composed solely of severe Japanese monks. Earnest seekers of truth from many countries and cultures, both male and female, traditional and modern, struggled silently. Roshi Shibayama left a unique request with Keido Fukushima, his youngest spiritual descendant, and there, kneeling on the hard wooden floor, was the proof of fulfillment. Following in the wake of decades of devotion and hard work, the true spirit of Zen was coming to the West.

> *Toku wa ko narazu*
> *Kanarazu*
> *Tonari ari*
> (Virtue is not alone, but always has neighbors.)

Hap Tivey
Bard College

*

* * *

I had the privilege of being Keido Fukushima's English teacher for one full year, when he came to Claremont, California, in 1972. He had been sent by his Master—Roshi Shibayama—not only to brush up on his English so that he could help westerners understand Zen, but also to learn about America itself. For one year, then, I would meet with him and help him with English and also take him to various places in southern California that seemed to me "American." These ranged from Baskin Robbins ice-cream parlors, through movie theatres where we saw films such as "The Sound of Music," to Benedictine monasteries where we could see monastic life, Christian style. As we did these things together, I taught him about English and about the United States, and he taught me about Zen.

His teachings took many forms, some of which were verbal. I will always remember the first time I met him. I had been taught that in Japan people bow, and he had been taught that in the United States people shake hands, so our first actual encounter was the experience of having his outstretched hand on my forehead. I am sure that we were both a little nervous, but this non-verbal event certainly broke the ice, at least for him. He laughed immediately, and I realized that, whatever Zen was, it was not simply about being serious all the time. It was obedience to the call of the moment, and this moment called for laughter.

After we entered the apartment where he was staying— Blaisdell House—he asked in broken English if I might like some coffee. He had figured out how to make it. As he made the coffee, I thought to myself: What will I say to this Zen priest? After all, it was all new to me. He brought me the coffee, after which I thought I would try to make conversation. I asked him how his trip went, and he answered, "Fine." Then, for some strange reason, I blurted out, in a deeply serious way: "Tell me, what do you know as a Zen person that I don't?" I had been reading so much about Buddhism and about *nirvana* that I figured he knew something I didn't know, and I wanted him to tell me. Without any hesitation, he said to me: "I know that I am you, and you are me, too. But you don't know that." This, then, was a second lesson in Zen for me. It was that obedience to the call of the moment comes from a prior awareness that things aren't so separate in the first place. We can be outside each other's bodies, but inside each other's awareness, and the latter is closer to the real nature of things.

There were many other moments like this. There was the time, for example, when he spotted a black Labrador retriever happily strolling across a yard with a bone in his mouth and oblivious to any artificial conventions. Keido turned to me quickly and said: "Jay, do you see that dog?" I said, "Yes," and he responded, "That's a Zen master!" This helped me see that Zen cherishes something deep and spontaneous and natural within the human mind, and that maybe old Joshu's dog did indeed have the Buddha nature after all. And there was the time when, after we got up from a table and walked to the door of a room where we were sitting, he looked back where he had been sitting and said: "Jay, do you remember that Zen priest back there?" I said, "Yes," and he pointed to himself at that moment and said, "New Zen priest!" This helped me see that Zen is about every moment being a new moment.

And then there was the *zazen* itself, when I would sit with Keido, somehow feeling the strength of his own sitting, and somehow feeling a pipeline between him and the others who were sitting, filled with contagious silence. These moments, too, were teachings, albeit in a more "letting go" way. But then again, almost all the things I did with my "student" were teachings for me, and now, so many years later, I find my mind filled with such memories. Added to them, though, is the fact that we have remained friends ever since, and that we see each other once a year, when he visits the college where I teach. And added to them is the retreat he leads, in which I am a participant, amid which I do *dokusan* with him (the asking and responding to Zen questions). Of course, I am not sure I will ever truly know the sound of one hand clapping. I'm not sure I'll ever clap back in just the right way. But what is so clear to me, even now, is that there is a rather deep friendship between the two of us that transcends many, many dualisms, including that of him being "Buddhist" and me being "Christian." I will always appreciate that, in this friendship, I never for a moment sensed that I was supposed to become Buddhist in order to learn from him and with him. Nor do I to this day. Our relationship runs much deeper than Buddhist-Christian dialogue. It is Buddhist-Christian friendship, and beyond that, too. Just friends ... like old dogs, running across a lawn, each with their bones.

Jay McDaniel
Professor of Religion
Hendrix College

*

* * *

How am I to respond to an invitation to share my "impressions" of Keido Fukushima, Chief Abbot of Tofukuji monastery? An impression obviously means that something has exerted pressure and left a mark. Although the monastic discipline of life at Tofukuji is closed to women, he nonetheless opens the gate when he can, and inspires discipleship in both men and women, even far beyond those walls. The mark of his passage into my life has left its own unique traces.

He came to us at the Institute for Medieval Japanese Studies in New York in 1993 by a blessed connection. It was an historical accident, I think, yet predestined. The Zen nun Mugai Nyodai (1223-1298 C.E.), early on, before she had become the eminent founding abbess of a "Five Mountain" convent, had gone to Tofukuji seeking to study with its founder, the monk Shoichi Kokushi (Ben'en), but was belittled by his monk-disciples and was forced to retreat. The centuries change. But spirits from the past move us. I think she knew it was time to send Tofukuji's abbot to us, to a place where abbess Mugai Nyodai has become our patron saint. And he came not only to talk of Zen and show the way of *zazen* and calligraphy; he offers up *sutra*s to the memory of abbess Mugai Nyodai each time he comes.

I am not a "Buddhist," whatever that is. Born into a Quaker family in Philadelphia, I learned in that meditative faith, too, that there is neither priest nor lay, neither master nor disciple. I say "too" because one Zen phrase abbot Fukushima writes often with his brush is "*muhinju*" ("There is here neither guest nor host"). Profoundly moved by his expositions on *muhinju* as well as on the phrase "*Nichi nichi kore ko nichi*" ("Every single day is a good day"), I hung his calligraphed renditions of these words in the entrance hall of our little research center in Kyoto just founded this year (2003). Invariably the eyes of each visitor strike these words as they enter; like visual bells they sound out and set the tone of our sacred space.

Abbot Fukushima usually comes to us in New York in February or March. Snowstorms shut down airports; hurricane-floods close down highways into Manhattan. Yet people come to hear him no matter what.

Each university he visits has a unique personality. He comes each year to Columbia where the numbers are modest, always students and seekers, almost never scholars. The numbers are modest because scholars, in the thrall of reason, still treasure the illusory high arrogance inherent to our trade, which values texts over and above the buddhas who live those texts today. We scholars spend our youth trying to develop the rational mind. I was one, trained and compressed into the mold. I grow yearly more ashamed. And yet not ashamed. "*Kashikoku nare*" ("To be smart") is *not* a Zen phrase.

For a decade now he has come to New York, like Bodhidharma (Daruma) on a mission abroad, to expose those who suffer to the message of Zen and to the existence of Bodhidharma. To me, however, Daruma's portraits always look ferocious, worried, and full of fret and fume. There is an essential truth, however, to the title of this present book by Ishwar Harris, *The Laughing Buddha*. Every time we meet I am struck anew by the joy that abbot Fukushima's presence seems to spread. His whole self smiles unself-consciously. Take a look at the frontispiece photo of the abbot in Jason Wirth's *Zen no sho*. Even when the corners of Keido Fukushima's mouth turn down like Daruma's, his eyes are laughing.

As mentioned above, we opened a new Center for the Study of Women, Buddhism, and Cultural History in a tiny convent residence on Teramachi-dori in Kyoto. The little house could not have come to us had not abbot Fukushima lent me his stead-fast optimism and faith throughout the past ten years, since the time such a place was hardly more than a thin moonbeam of hope. When we received the little house from Daishoji abbess Kasanoin Jikun-sama, there was a tiny barren space just outside the entry door. "It is no bigger than a *tatami* mat, a desolate strip of earth at the foot of a concrete wall. Can you help me turn it into a beautiful and meaningful spot?" I asked. He sent me his own gardener from Sone Zoen, and with a scant bushel of white sand, a few good stones, and a bit of moss, a new world was born there.

"Don't over-water the moss," the gardener said. "Moss knows by itself how to drink from the air." I was struck wordless. I took it as a Zen teaching. For the first time I understood the words *"Ikioi, tsukai-tsukusu bekarazu"* (No need to expend *all* one's energy). Even moss inherently knows buddhahood. In our small patch of moss, the footprints, everlasting, of Fukushima roshi.

Barbara Ruch
Director, Institute of Medieval Japanese Studies
Professor Emerita
Japanese Literature and Culture
Columbia University

*
* * *

Roshi Fukushima first became known to me thirty years ago when I was teaching at Notre Dame Seishin Women's University in Okayama from 1973-1974. At that time Roshi was at Hofukuji Monastery in Soja City in the countryside of Okayama province. There were three American men who were studying Zen with him and when I showed an interest in joining them on occasion for *zazen* he welcomed me to the monastery. From the very beginning of our meeting Roshi was cordial and gracious in every way. At the time I did not fully realize how unusual it was to have an American woman join these *zazen* sessions. Over the years my appreciation for this openness has deepened as Roshi has continued to be a remarkable bridge to the West for Rinzai Zen. As a teacher he is unique—full of wisdom and insight but also humor and compassion. He has a breadth of human understanding that is rare, yet readily perceptible by all who meet him.

Twenty years later when Roshi began to visit campuses in the States in the early 1990s he started coming to Bucknell each year as part of his trip. It has been a great joy to receive him at Bucknell as well as at Harvard and at Berkeley when my husband and I were at these universities on sabbatical. His skill in speaking to students and in leading Zen retreats with them is remarkable. They talk about his visit for months (indeed years) afterward.

In addition, my husband and I have had the good fortune to visit Roshi on a number of occasions in Kyoto at Tofukuji. These have been the high points of our trips to Japan. From the moment one walks across the bridge at Tofukuji one knows one is in another world and a special kind of peacefulness arises. This is amplified when one is in the presence of Roshi, who puts visitors at ease immediately. I will never forget his graciousness in receiving many foreign visitors who attended the conference of the Global Forum in 1993 and again when we had a special interreligious dialogue with a Shinto leader and a Confucian scholar at Tofukuji. The sincerity and warmth of Roshi is boundless and my gratitude to him is beyond words. He has touched my life in more ways than I can ever fully say and his influence will be with me all the days of my life.

Mary Evelyn Tucker
Department of Religion
Bucknell University
Lewisburg PA

*

* * *

My friendship with Keido Fukushima began with an art exhibition. Yet this was already something quite different from what I had expected when growing up. From my early years I was sure that my life would be in music, and after graduating from college I set out to be a composer in my hometown of New York City. I soon discovered that life is not all planning, however; serendipity also plays an important part. First, I had the opportunity to study experimental composition with John Cage, who had been a pupil of D. T. Suzuki at Columbia, and who embodied many aspects of Zen in his own unique way. Second, a friend from high school days named Bill Crofut invited me to join him in a folk music tour of Asia, and although I was composing pieces in the classical mode, I dusted off my guitar in 1961 for what I thought would be a few months. These few months lasted seventeen years. I discovered that learning about different cultures through their songs and instruments was fascinating, and we came back to America to share what we had learned, then toured in other countries several times again.

During our tours I became especially interested in East Asian culture, for reasons I did not yet understand. One day in Tokyo I happened to look through the window of an art shop and saw a Zen painting hanging on a wall. Something clicked; I went into the shop to inquire and spent hours looking at scrolls and trying to make sense of what I was being told. Since the dealer knew no English and I did not speak Japanese at the time, this was seemingly futile, but it didn't matter, I was fascinated. Meanwhile, the "folk music boom" of the 1960s boosted our career as "Addiss and Crofut," and we made a number of records and appeared on various television shows at that time. We especially enjoyed performing at full concerts where we had time to compare our own songs with music we had learned in Asia and Africa. Eventually, however, I realized that I needed more formal study of Asian culture and languages, so I went back to school for M.A. and Ph.D. degrees in East Asian music and art, and began to teach, mostly Japanese art, at the University of Kansas. During the year of 1988 I was completing work for a book and exhibit entitled "The Art of Zen: Paintings and Calligraphy by Japanese Monks, 1600-1900." We received a generous grant from the National Endowment for the Humanities for this exhibition, including funds for an "artist in residence." Since Zen masters rather than professional painters and calligraphers do Zen art, it seemed to me that we had little chance of utilizing this fund, but it was certainly worth the effort to try.

One of my Ph.D. students named Matthew Welch was in Kyoto at that time, working on his dissertation about a Zen monk-artist named Nantembo Toju (1839-1925), so I wrote to Matthew to ask if he had any suggestions. It turned out that he had meditated at Tofukuji under Roshi Fukushima, who was not only a leading Zen master but also a fine calligrapher. At my request, Matthew enquired of Fukushima if he might be interested in coming to the Spencer Museum of Art in Lawrence, Kansas, during the time of our exhibition. When the Roshi replied that it might be possible, I journeyed to Japan in late November 1988, to discuss the project in person. This was my first meeting with Roshi Fukushima, and I will never forget it. The last of the wondrous autumn leaves at Tofukuji were still showing their splendor, and the weather was cool and crisp. The Roshi treated me with great kindness, showing a great interest in my work. He explained that he had spent a good deal of time in the United States in his younger days, but reestablishing the Zen training center at Tofukuji had meant that he could not return for some years. With the *zendo* now functioning well, he was willing to contemplate a visit to us, but what exactly would we ask of him? I said that we hoped he would give several talks about Zen, and also do public demonstrations of Zen calligraphy. He replied that although he did not do such demonstrations in Japan, he might be willing to show his brushwork in America because it would be appropriate for the Zen art exhibition. He was also kind enough at that time to assist me in the reading of one of the works of Zen calligraphy in the exhibition, a phrase that had eluded several major scholars of Buddhism. I was extremely happy with his generosity, and we made plans for his visit in the spring of 1989.

Roshi Fukushima was an amazing success in Kansas. His talks were well attended and well received since he had the gift of speaking in a lively, fresh, and meaningful way to each audience, whether adults, students, or young children. In addition, his calligraphy demonstrations were spellbinding; people who had seen one came back for another, and the crowds grew until the museum's center court was absolutely full of people, including viewers hanging over the balcony above him. Watching him meditate briefly before each work, then move his brush quickly, dramatically, and with full control down the paper was an experience that reached everyone, whether or not they had any knowledge about Zen. Fukushima later explained that he did not intend to give such demonstrations again, but when he saw how well they communicated with the public, he realized that they helped to build a bridge between Japan and the United States, not only from one culture to another, but also from one heart and mind to another.

Since I went to all of his public talks and demonstrations, I noticed that the Roshi never gave the same comments, although he could easily have repeated his words to different audiences. I mentioned to him that his talks were always different, but just as I said this I realized, and said, that they were also always the same, meaning that what lay underneath the words was absolutely consistent. He apparently liked this comment, and went on to tell the next group of people that I had said his talks were always different, but always the same. His translator put this in English backwards, "always the same but always different." Roshi Fukushima, with his excellent English, noticed this and insisted that the translation was incorrect, it should be "always different and always the same."

I believe that this phrase explains a good deal about how Zen can move through time and space, from China to Japan to the western world over the course of many centuries, and remain vital and meaningful. Roshi Fukushima has been a living example of this phrase, responding to each person at each moment in that combination of freedom and responsibility that marks his Zen mind and personal character.

Since then I have had the yearly privilege of visiting the Roshi at Tofukuji and welcoming him to Kansas, and now to the University of Richmond. He has greatly helped my studies of Zen and Zen art, and I was delighted to assist Professor Audrey Yoshiko Seo, now my wife, when she prepared a sequel in 1998 to our first exhibition, called "The Art of Twentieth-Century Zen." This exhibit and book concluded with Audrey's chapter about Fukushima's teacher Zenkei Shibayama and then Fukushima himself, and once again his visits to the United States were able to coincide with this exhibition at various venues including the Japan Society Gallery in New York City and the Los Angeles County Museum. It has also been the pleasure of Dr. Seo and myself to write catalogue chapters for the 2003 exhibition of Fukushima's calligraphy, "*Zen no Sho*," organized by Oglethorpe University in Atlanta.

It is difficult to explain how much the friendship of Roshi Fukushima has meant to me over the years. Certainly I have learned a great deal about Japanese culture, about Zen, and about Zen art from him, and I much enjoy studying a Zen text or calligraphy with him, but his warmth, humor, and generosity of spirit have meant even more. I notice that even college freshmen somehow understand that there is something remarkable about him, even if they merely see him walking from classroom to classroom; he radiates a special quality that goes beyond words.

As the world becomes smaller, Fukushima's bridge between Japan and the United States is increasingly important, but his influence goes much further. All those who know him have felt the impact of his wisdom, whether or not they meditate, go to Tofukuji for special training sessions, or just find more discipline, understanding, joy, and freedom in their own lives. I am very grateful that the path of my life has crossed so happily and productively with Roshi Fukushima, and I wish nothing less for all those who can meet him, see him, hear him, or simply view his calligraphy, the ink traces that will exist far into the future to express his Zen Mind.

Stephen Addiss
Tucker-Boatwright Professor
University of Richmond

*
* * *

We here at Xavier University consider ourselves among the lucky ones. For over ten years now, Roshi Keido Fukushima (or simply "Roshi" as our students call him) has been paying a yearly visit to our university community, giving talks, providing calligraphy demonstrations, and offering a weekend Zen retreat. But to capture the focus of my impressions of him, and the particular sparkle in my friendship with him, I have to look back to a visit my family and I paid him at his Tofukuji monastery in January 1991.

My wife Cathy and I were there with our two children, John (then 14) and Moira (11). Roshi provided us with a splendid, multi-course, multi-colored Zen lunch. There we sat on the floor of a beautiful visitors' dining room, the Roshi on one side of a square low-lying table and the four of us on the other, as two young monks carried in course after exotic course of Zen-Japanese delicacies. And as the monks entered and then bowed out of the room, the muffled remarks of Moira grew more anguished and more perceptible: "Yuk! What is that? Looks like seaweed. I can't eat that. Can we stop at MacDonald's on the way back to the hotel?" And the more difficult it became for me to camouflage my embarrassed and very un-Zenlike reaction to her: "Be quiet. Eat as much as you can. And smile."

And there on the other side of the table sat the Roshi, his warm smile matching Moira's distress and my awkward embarrassment. He knew exactly what was going on. And he seemed silently, sensitively, to delight in it. Moira was being who and what little girls often are. And Roshi accepted—yes, seemed to delight in—just that. It never disturbed the flow of his conversation with us.

This, for me, is what warms me in my relationship with him. He is fully present to, fully accepting of, and fully responsive to, everyone he meets. No matter how much activity or talking may be going on around the crowded conference hall or dinner table, when you talk to him, or he to you, you feel that there is no one else there. With his attention and compassion and smile, he is there for you. Whether it's a squirming little girl who doesn't like seaweed or a retreatant with an inappropriate question, he is there and no where else.

If I can be allowed a Zen reflection: he can do this because he perceives, responds to, and nourishes the Buddha-nature in each one of us, at whatever moment in our lives. He has shown me that if every day is a fine day, every person entering my life is a Buddha-person.

I am grateful, very grateful, for his friendship.

Paul F. Knitter
Professor Emeritus of Theology
Xavier University
Cincinnati, Ohio, USA

*
* * *

I first met Keido Fukushima in early 1989 when he made his first visit to the University of Kansas in conjunction with the exhibition "The Art of Zen," which had been organized by Professor

Stephen Addiss. Much later I learned the story of how he had been brought to the university, of the curator of education telling Dr. Addiss and the Spencer's curator of Asian art, Pat Fister, "And of course we'll have a Zen monk lecture and demonstrate calligraphy," and of Addiss and Fister saying, "Where are we going to find a Zen monk who will do that?" One of our graduate students, Matthew Welch, was meditating at Tofukuji and he suggested that the Roshi might be willing to come. And that was how the wonderful relationship between Kansas University and Tofukuji developed.

When the Roshi first came to Kansas University I had no background in Japanese art or culture and no special personal interest in Zen. I had never really thought about it. But when he was in the museum, staff members would disappear from their offices when he gave a presentation or class. And people seemed to be inspired by something he was doing. I finally attended his calligraphy demonstration and was completely amazed at the freedom with which he wrote and the similarities it seemed to have with the way American abstract expressionist painters worked. A person who was there with me that first time later told me the lecture had changed her life.

The Roshi kept returning to Kansas. After attending many of his lectures and demonstrations, I began to have a sense of how Zen Buddhism could affect one's worldview and activities. At his meditation sessions he made suggestions as to how even brief periods of meditation, practicing "empty mind," could refresh one for one's studies or work. It took me years to realize the central role of *mu* in his talks and practice and even longer to realize he began every demonstration with *mu*.

A few years ago some members of the staff began to adopt the Roshi's saying, "Every day is a fine day," sometimes said ruefully. Oddly, every time we would say it, we would realize that the statement was, in fact, true. Keido Fukushima has subtly and gradually affected our worldview and begun to instill in us a vision of peace and acceptance.

Some years ago I made my first trip to Japan and in Kyoto and elsewhere the Roshi made me his guest. One could not have a better introduction to the art and culture of Japan. In Kyoto he is subtly different from the way he is in the United States, where people see his self referential humor and tend to find him funny. In Japan his power, his responsibility as head of Tofukuji, and the deep reverence and respect people feel for him are more fully visible, making it doubly impressive that he is so accessible to us in Kansas. It was during that first trip to Japan that I learned something about his life, his practice, his values, and his generosity. For months after that and again whenever I visit, I see his powerful smile and feel cheered and reassured. "Every day is a fine day."

Andrea S. Norris
Director, Spencer Museum of Art
The University of Kansas

*

* * *

For many visitors to Tofukuji Monastery, the western style guest room where they first meet Roshi Fukushima is the site of many fond memories. Replete with comfortable sofas, large windows, curious artifacts, and the only heating/cooling systems in the whole building, it is a light and airy place with a generously welcoming ambience. Far fewer guests, however, ever see the nearby *dokusan* (Zen question and answer) room—a small, stark space with only a purple cushion and incense stand on the floor. Its size hints at an intimacy between a master and disciple in which either may use words or actions to reveal the state of their being, but the room's forbidding austerity implicitly situates such free-form expression within the boundaries of Rinzai Zen's formalized traditions.

As a former monk who spent many hours in both locations, the physical proximity between the two rooms is more than a matter of architectural detail. Taken in tandem, they aptly reflect two distinct, yet intertwined facets of the man whose presence defines the tenor of Tofukuji's position in modern Zen practice. In my mind, the Roshi of the guestroom is a jovial figure with a quick wit and a true passion for entertaining friends and other visitors. His openness is particularly manifest in his willingness to greet westerners with an interest in Zen. This is a rare trait among modern Japanese monastery abbots, and it is indicative of his belief that Zen is not only accessible to Japanese, but to all practitioners. The Roshi of the *dokusan* room, though, is a more imposing personage. Silent and unmoving, his joviality is replaced by severity, and he becomes a barrier that every disciple must pass. While always a mirror of his individual humanity, the Roshi's *dokusan* persona also manifests his sense of responsibility to his tradition as an embodiment of its centuries-old method for religious and spiritual pedagogy.

I have always been struck by the way Roshi Fukushima maintains a balance between this adamantine faith in the traditions of Rinzai Zen, and his willingness to contravene some of the cultural and institutional conventions that define traditional Japanese monasticism when dealing with a western audience. This balance is exemplified in his insistence that western practitioners fully understand the meaning of "Roshi" in Rinzai practice, and his policy of allowing western women to perform *zazen* in the *zendo*, a hall that is usually off-limits to women. This duality derives both from his acceptance of differences between Japanese and American culture, and his desire to enunciate a baseline for establishing a model of Rinzai Zen authority that can transcend cultural boundaries. Ultimately, I believe his role as a progressive-traditional Zen master will mark his legacy in the history of Japanese and American Zen practice.

Alexander Vesey
Stonehill College

*

* * *

After many years, I am finally beginning to see the wide variety of blind selves that I have presented to Roshi Fukushima! The patience he must have!

Since I received the blessing of an introduction to him from my professor at Pomona, Peggy Dornish, he has guided me from wide-eyed wonder through disillusionment, reluctant acceptance, bullheaded injury, commitment, and on to the inklings of an understanding of the simplicity of Zen practice.

In my profession, as in most fields, it is an extremely rare event to meet an artist who is both a dynamic performer and an inspiring teacher. Roshi Fukushima is a man who can articulately explain the artistry of the Zen life he is demonstrating to you right now. He can do it in Japanese, or English.

A True Master.

> With love,
> Tim Armacost
> Jazz Musician
> New York

*
* * *

I first encountered Zen Buddhism in a world religions course, which prompted me to explore the religion further in an upper level course titled "Zen and the Arts in Japanese Culture." While reading texts on Zen by D. T. Suzuki and other Zen gurus, I was rather mystified with explanations of "Zen is not this…. Zen is not that…." What is Zen? I caught a glimpse of "what Zen is" upon meeting Roshi Fukushima when he lectured on Zen and demonstrated Zen calligraphy on my college campus. I suppose I expected the Zen master to be stern and disciplined or perhaps constantly absorbed in meditation. However, as he walked into the auditorium, an aura of both peacefulness and enthusiasm for life radiated from him. This effect on the audience was accomplished without words and was experienced directly by those in his presence. He began the lecture with a glowing smile and a humorous statement about how he was going to race my professor in a wheelchair race at old age. While his explanation of Zen and demonstration of calligraphy was reciprocated well by the western audience, it was the Zen master himself who conveyed the message of Zen. The art, philosophy, and intellectual endeavors are manifestations of Zen, but not Zen itself. Zen, as conveyed by the Roshi, was the experience of everyday life. Likewise, the monastic practices, which had consumed my understanding of Zen, seemed now to be merely devices—fingers pointing at the moon, but not the moon itself. While I do not understand Zen in an experiential way, I realize that it is a way of life.

Learning that I was to study abroad in Japan the following year, the Roshi gave me his *meishi* (business card) and invited me to visit the monastery in Kyoto. Thus, I traveled to Kyoto for a weekend visit with my mother and sister (who were visiting me in Tokyo). We were very interested in visiting the monastery, but I hesitated to call the Roshi because of the short notice. To my dismay, he offered not only to let us tour the monastery, but sent his car and driver to pick us up at our hotel that day. We were greeted in the hotel lobby by a monk who led us to the car and the driver then took us to the back entrance of the monastery. We were led to the Roshi's quarters where we talked to him for over two hours! He explained the core principles of Zen Buddhism and everyday monastic life to us. We were taken aback by his overwhelming kindness, his shuffling of his own schedule to accommodate our visit. Once again, I was struck by his sense of humor, which seems almost "unorthodox" for such an authoritative religious figure; and then, once again, there was a glimpse of the Zen experience. Afterward, a monk led us on a leisurely tour of the monastery. I will always remember this visit to the monastery and the extraordinary kindness of Roshi Fukushima.

Ginny Miraldi
Class of 2003
The College of Wooster

*
* * *

The gold threads glistening on Roshi's overlay were the first thing that caught my attention during his lecture to hundreds of students in our college auditorium. When we met following the lecture, I inquired about the beautiful, decorative cloth covering his simple, monotone robe. He immediately took it off and placed it on my shoulders before explaining the significance of the richly embroidered fabric. I was surprised by Roshi's humor and ability to rise above his grand appearance. The magnificent look of his clothing suggested a facade that could easily disguise Roshi's open and friendly manner.

Our second meeting occurred at Tofukuji Monastery in Kyoto, Japan where I was fortunate to spend a few days participating in the monks' meditation routines. Roshi spoke to me informally, telling jokes and sharing stories about his travels around the world and the monasteries under his care. He made a lasting impression on me when he took the time to ask questions about my interests. Roshi sought to learn from each person with whom he came in contact as much as he strived to impart his wealth of knowledge to others. I recognized this more as Roshi instructed the monks to teach me all of the ceremonies concerning the meditation sessions and meals. They meticulously informed me of each detail associated with the ceremonies. Although it might seem they were only concerned that I become indoctrinated with the tenets of Zen Buddhism, they were eager to absorb all I shared with them about my way of life.

Roshi's life at the monastery and abroad is governed by strict rules and a tight schedule, but this stern order gives him the freedom to enjoy life as much as possible. These rules and regulations free him from daily routine concerns and let him focus on more important ideas and thoughts about other aspects of life and the community that surrounds him. Roshi encouraged me to focus on the people around me and to live in harmony with them by soaking up the knowledge that can be shared between us.

Hannalori Bates
Class of 2003
The College of Wooster

*

* * *

Keido Fukushima and I first met in the summer of 1982. He had become the Roshi or Zen master at the Tofukuji monks' training hall in 1980. I had arrived in Japan in the summer of 1981 and spent my first year getting my toes wet at Myoshinji, another one of the major Rinzai Zen monasteries.

One of the things that inspired me to come to Japan and throw myself into a monastery was reading *Zen Comments on the Mumonkan* by Zenkei Shibayama (recently republished by Shambhala as *The Gateless Barrier*). To this day, it remains one of the very few reliable books in English on *koan* practice.

When I first met Roshi Fukushima he told me that he had trained at Nanzenji under Roshi Shibayama, who passed away in 1974. With that, our mutual fate was sealed, although at the time I had no idea how entwined were our lives. For just like Fukushima, I had spent years in graduate school learning about Zen before despairing of academic study, and we both finally entered the monastery at the relatively late age of twenty-eight. As I was soon to learn, Shibayama had told his disciple to train Americans. Roshi Fukushima, now in his early seventies, has worked tirelessly to do this, making Japanese Rinzai Zen available to the world despite nearly endless requests of every imaginable kind.

In the early 1990s I accompanied him as interpreter and assistant for four annual tours of the United States. Instead of just fifteen or twenty seconds in the formal *koan* practice known as *dokusan* or *sanzen*, this was a precious opportunity to spend day in and day out with him and see him as a human being, foibles and all. Thus I was forced to take him down from the pedestal I had unconsciously put him on—an important though unexpected facet of my practice. No problem for him—though it was for me at the time!

He would often take time out of his busy schedule in the United States to buy presents for children, whom he adores. Giving the gifts, he was as overjoyed as the kids were. It brought home the truth of the expression that, in selfless giving, there truly is "neither guest nor host"—just beaming faces all around.

His ever-smiling face in the States contrasts sharply with his role as Zen master at the monastery, a fact that sometimes surprises and shocks visitors who have no idea how fortunate they are to be able to join in monastic practice at Tofukuji. To give some idea just how precious this is, an American friend who had done retreats in several Zen centers in the States, both Soto and Rinzai, after only one day of a *sesshin*-retreat at Tofukuji concluded that he had done more Zen practice in that day than in the last twenty-five years.

What, finally, has Roshi Fukushima taught? For over twenty years I have been practicing under him. But what has he taught me? Here his greatness as a *koan* master really shines forth. I cannot stress enough that in the *dokusan* or *sanzen* room he never taught a thing. For his severe and uncompromising demeanor I am profoundly grateful. He demands, as he should—as he must—that we dig it out of ourselves.

Now it is up to us to bring it to life in our world. He wants nothing more. Thus we repay our incalculable debt to innumerable Buddhas and Patriarchs.

Gasshou (Palms Pressed Together),

Jeff Shore
Lay Zen man
Professor of International Zen
Hanazono University
Kyoto, Japan

Roshi Keido Fukushima

Glossary

avidya: a Sanskrit term used both in Hinduism and Buddhism to denote the state of "ignorance." The opposite of *avidya* is *vidya*, which is "knowledge" leading to emancipation.

Bhagavadgita: known as the Bible of the Hindus, it is considered to be one of the most popular of all Hindu texts. It describes the ways of liberation as taught by Krishna to his friend, Arjuna.

Bodhidharma: the 28th patriarch of Buddhism and the 1st patriarch of Zen, he is said to have brought the meditation school of Buddhism to China around 520 C.E. A legendary figure whose face is painted by many Zen masters.

boku-seki: a Japanese term used to describe Zen calligraphy. It is different from *zenga*, which is secular calligraphy. Most Zen masters are fond of producing *boku-seki* to illustrate the insights of Zen.

Butsu-dan: a small shrine dedicated to the Buddha. Usually found in Buddhist homes, it serves as the family altar.

Dhammapada: a collection of 423 verses, composed in Pali, giving the foundation of Buddhist moral philosophy; considered to be a central text of Sakyamuni Buddha's teaching.

dhyana: a Sanskrit term meaning "meditation." In China it was pronounced as "Ch'an," and in Japan it became "Zen."

dokusan: a Japanese term whose literal meaning is "go alone"; in Rinzai Zen it refers to the meeting of the disciple with the Zen master for the purpose of *koan* practice.

Eiheiji: one of the two head temples of the Soto Zen sect, it is located in the deep mountains near Fukui City. It was founded by Dogen Zenji in 1243 C.E.

haiku: a 17 syllable Japanese style of poetry.

Hakuin: (1685-1768 C.E.), renowned Japanese master of Rinzai Zen.

ikebana: flower arrangement.

jikijitsu: the head monk in charge of the meditation hall in a Zen monastery.

ji yu: freedom.

Joshu (Chin. Chao-chou): (778-897 C.E.), one of the earliest and greatest of the Chinese Zen masters. He is well known for his answer of "*mu*" to the question, "Does a dog have Buddha-nature?"

kancho: head abbot.

karuna: a Sanskrit term meaning "compassion"; considered to be one of the pillars of faith and at the heart of Buddhist teachings.

keishaku: a long flat stick carried by the monk in charge during sitting meditation. It is used to strike those meditating in order to encourage them in the discipline of concentration. To receive a blow is considered an honor.

kensho: to see the Buddha-nature; to attain *satori*.

koan: a Japanese word used to describe a phrase or a statement that cannot be solved by the intellect. In Rinzai Zen tradition, *koan*s are used to awaken the intuitive mind.

Mahakasyapa: a famous disciple of the Sakyamuni Buddha. He is said to have understood the secret of the flower, which the Buddha had held in his hand without giving a sermon.

Maitreya: the Buddha of the future who will inaugurate a reign of peace and harmony in the midst of suffering. In the Far East, he is depicted as the potbellied Buddha.

Mara: a Sanskrit term that literally means "death"; the personification of evil in Buddhist mythology. He is said to have tempted the Buddha as he meditated under the bodhi tree.

maya: a Sanskrit term used in Hindu tradition to denote that all phenomenal reality is appearance. The only real reality is Brahman, the Absolute One.

mondo: a Japanese term translated as "questions and answers" to denote dialogues between a Zen master and his disciples. Some of the *mondo*s became the basis for *koan*s.

Mt. Koya: center of Shingon (Japanese esoteric) Buddhism; located in Wakayama prefecture; founded by Kukai (Kobo Daishi, 774-835 C.E.) in 816 C.E.

mu: a Japanese term used to describe a non-ego self. The goal in Zen is to become *mu-no-hito*, a person without ego.

mushin: a Japanese term used to describe the Zen state of no-mind. Roshi Keido Fukushima likes to describe it as "creative mind," "free mind," or "open mind." The goal of Zen is to achieve and function in this state of mind which transcends all dualities.

Nagarjuna: a Buddhist philosopher and saint usually placed in the beginning of the second century C.E. He taught

Shunyavada, meaning that all reality is empty of any permanent essence. His thought is central to Zen philosophy.

Nanzenji: located in Kyoto, Japan, it is a training monastery and the head temple of the Nanzenji school of the Rinzai sect of Buddhism.

nirguna Brahman: a Sanskrit term to describe the Ultimate Reality (Brahman) without qualities. Also known as the Unmanifest Reality as discussed in the Vedanta school of Hinduism.

nyoi: a small stick carried by a Zen master; a symbol of the master's authority.

paticcasamuppada: a Pali word in Theravada Buddhism which is usually translated as "dependent co-origination"; describes the process by which a being comes into existence, and which binds the individual to the wheel of life.

prajna: a Sanskrit term that denotes transcendental wisdom. It is considered one of the most important pillars of Mahayana Buddhism, including Zen.

Radhakrishnan, S.: (1888-1975 C.E.), an eminent Hindu philosopher and a prolific writer, who is known for interpreting Hinduism to the west.

Rinzai (Chin. Lin-chi): (d. 867 C.E.), renowned Chinese Zen master and founder of the Rinzai sect. His teachings are contained in the *Lin-chi Records*.

rohatsu: a Japanese term referring to a weeklong retreat (*sesshin*) held by Japanese Zen monasteries. From the early morning of December first to early morning of December eighth, the participants participate in this intensive weeklong retreat without lying down.

Ryokan: (1758-1831 C.E.), Zen master of the Soto sect.

saguna Brahman: a Sanskrit term to describe the Ultimate Reality (Brahman) with qualities. Also known as the Manifest Reality as discussed in the Vedanta school of Hinduism.

saki: Japanese wine.

Sankhya: a Sanskrit term whose literal meaning is "distinction"; the name of one of the six orthodox schools of philosophy. It sees reality divided into two realms: *purusha* (spirit) and *prakriti* (matter). Both are deemed real; thus establishing a dualistic form of thought.

sanzen: *koan* study; also, more widely, the study of Zen.

satori: a Japanese term used to describe the enlightenment experience central to Zen. It is sometimes described as a flash of intuitive awareness, which is real but often incommunicable.

sensei: teacher.

sesshin: a weeklong intensive meditation session. In a Zen training monastery, several such sessions are held during the course of the year.

Sesshu: (1421-1506 C.E.), one of the great Zen teachers and painters known within the Zen tradition in Japan. Trained at Hofukuji, he went to China to study art and became one of the great artists of Japan.

Shankara: (788 - 820 C.E.), an exponent of the non-dualistic (*advaita*) school of Hinduism, who asserted that all Reality is One. An opponent of Indian Buddhism, he is also known as a crypto-Buddhist.

Shoichi: (1202-1280 C.E.), first Patriarch of Tofukuji.

shunyata: a Sanskrit term used to describe the state of voidness as discussed in the Madhyamika school of Nagarjuna, which became central to Zen experience.

skandhas: a Sanskrit term used to describe the absence of a permanent self; it usually refers to the five aggregates, viz.: the body, feelings, perceptions, states of mind, and awareness—all of which are in a state of constant flux.

sodo: a Japanese word used to describe the monks' quarters within the monastery.

sumiye: ink painting.

teisho: a Japanese term used to describe the *dharma* talk that the Zen master gives to his disciples, monks, and to lay people.

Tenrikyo: one of the newer religions of Japan that came into existence on October 26, 1838. The Tenrikyo Church headquarters is located in the city of Tenri in central Japan. It holds that God the Parent, Tenri-o-no-Mikoto became revealed through a woman, Miki Nakayama, to save all humankind.

Theravada: an early form of Indian Buddhism translated as "The Teachings of the Elders." As a historical religious tradition, it was formed soon after the death of the Sakyamuni Buddha.

Tofukuji: located in Kyoto, Japan, it is a training monastery and the head temple of the Tofukuji school of the Rinzai sect of Buddhism.

Ummon: (864-949 C.E.), Chinese Zen (Ch'an) master.

Upanishads: among the sacred texts of the Hindus, most Upanishads discuss the existence of one absolute Reality known as Brahman. Much of Hindu Vedanta derives its inspiration from these texts.

zazen: a Japanese word used to describe sitting meditation practiced in Zen Buddhism.

zendo: the meditation hall, also used as the living quarters for the monks.

For a glossary of all key foreign words used in books published by World Wisdom, including metaphysical terms in English, consult:
www.DictionaryofSpiritualTerms.org.
This on-line Dictionary of Spiritual Terms provides extensive definitions, examples and related terms in other languages.

Roshi Keido Fukushima

Biographical Notes

ISHWAR C. HARRIS is Synod Professor of Religious Studies at the College of Wooster, where he has taught since 1981. Dr. Harris received his bachelor's degree from the Lucknow Christian College in India, his master's of divinity from the Howard Divinity School, his S.T.M. from the Pacific School of Religion, and his Ph.D. from Claremont Graduate School. A specialist in Eastern Religions, he is a member of the American Academy of Religion, the Society for Asian Studies, ASIANetwork, and the Ohio Academy of Religion. Dr. Harris is renowned for his in-depth knowledge of Hinduism, Buddhism, and Islam, and is an acknowledged expert on India's culture and civilization. His publications include: *Gandhians in Contemporary India: The Vision and the Visionaries* and *Radhakrishnan: Profile of a Universalist.*

Dr. Harris has had extensive personal contact with Keido Fukushima, head abbot of the Tofukuji Monastery in Kyoto. In the summer of 1999, he spent five weeks in Japan at the Tofukuji Monastery, where he meditated with the monks and observed their lifestyle under Roshi Fukushima. A further three-month trip to the monastery in 2001 and a shorter trip in 2003 allowed him to gather first-hand information from the Roshi and paved the way for his writing of *The Laughing Buddha of Tofukuji: The Life of Zen Master Keido Fukushima.*

JEFF SHORE is a lay Zen man and Professor of International Zen at Hanazono University, Kyoto, Japan, where he has taught since 1987. He received his MA in Comparative Philosophy from the University of Hawaii in 1978, focusing on Ch'an (Zen) Buddhism, and thereafter performed postgraduate work in the Department of Religion at Temple University, before he moved to Japan in 1981.

Professor Shore's writings include "The True Buddha is Formless: Masao Abe's Religious Quest," in *Masao Abe: A Zen Life of Dialogue* (ed. Donald W. Mitchell), entries for "Koan" and "Zen and the West" in *Encyclopedia of Monasticism* (ed. William M. Johnston), and "A Buddhist Model of the Human Self: Working Through the Jung-Hisamatsu Discussion," in *Awakening and Insight: Zen Buddhism and Psychotherapy* (eds. Polly Young-Eisendrath and Shoji Muramoto). He translated the novel *He's Leaving Home: My Young Son Becomes a Zen Monk*, by Kiyohiro Miura, winner of the prestigious Japanese Akutagawa literary prize in 1988.

He has studied and practiced Zen Buddhism for more than 30 years, spending over 20 years training under Keido Fukushima, head abbot of the Tofukuji training monastery in Kyoto. His annual retreats and lectures worldwide have been supported by grants from the Japanese Ministry of Education and the United States Department of Education.

Titles in the Spiritual Masters: East & West Series by World Wisdom